Nita Mehta's

VEGETARIAN

Punjabi

Vegetarian

Nita Mehta's

VEGETARIAN

Punjabi

COOKING

Nita Mehta

B.Sc. (Home Science), M.Sc. (Food and Nutrition), Gold Medalist

Tanya Mehta

SNAB
Publishers Pvt. Ltd.

Nita Mehta's
VEGETARIAN
Punjabi
COOKING

Reprint 2005

ISBN 81-7869-061-6

Food Styling & Photography: **SNAB**

Layout and laser typesetting:

National Information
Technology Academy
3A/3, Asaf Ali Road
New Delhi-110002
☎ 23252948

Published by:

SNAB
Publishers Pvt. Ltd.
3A/3 Asaf Ali Road,
New Delhi - 110002
Tel: 23252948, 23250091
Telefax:91-11-23250091

Editorial and Marketing office:
E-159, Greater Kailash-II, N.Delhi-48
Fax: 91-11-29225218, 29229558
Tel: 91-11-29214011, 29218727, 29218574
E-Mail: nitamehta@email.com
snab@snabindia.com
*Website:*http://www.nitamehta.com
Website: http://www.snabindia.com

Printed at:

BRIJBASI ART PRESS LTD.

Distributed by :

THE VARIETY BOOK DEPOT
A.V.G. Bhavan, M 3 Con Circus,
New Delhi - 110 001
Tel : 23417175, 23412567; Fax : 23415335
Email: varietybookdepot@rediffmail.com

Price: Rs. 195/-

Picture on cover: Lassi - Malai Maar Ke
Angoori Gajar Kofte
Poodina Parantha

Picture on page 1: *Til Mil Matar*

Picture on page 2: *Kele Aur Anjeer Ki Tikki*
Makai Vadi Chaska

Picture on Page 3: *Anjeer Halwa*

Picture on page 4: *Subziyaan Kali Mirch*

Picture on page 94: *Kamal Kakri Aur Aloo*
Dal Makhani

Picture on back cover: *Phool Tukri*

Introduction

Punjabi Khaana is much more than "*Makki Di Roti and Sarson Da Saag*". With plenty of food grains, dairy and vegetables, Punjabis dish out a variety of delectable vegetarian dishes. The book offers recipes which are sumptuous, yet not too rich as Punjabi Khaana is believed to be. The recipes have been carefully created to see that they are healthy as well as tasty.

Here we present a feast of delicacies ranging from thirst quenchers like Lassi, Kanji, Jeera, Sardai etc., to unusual sweet dishes like Channa Dal and Khajur ka Halwa, Anjeeri Kulfi, Cocogulla besides the ever green Kheer and Meethe Chaawal. The main course includes curries as well as dry and masala dishes.

A section on Snacks which includes Bhutte ke Pakore, Dahi Bhalle and many more will satisfy those empty in between meal moments. Finally to perk up the meals we have given the delicious Punjabi Mango Pickle *(am da achar)* and the Sweet and Sour Gobhi-Shalgam da Achar. With such a wide variety, offer your guests a grand spread of Punjabi Khaana.

Nita Mehta

ABOUT THE RECIPES

WHAT'S IN A CUP?

INDIAN CUP
1 teacup = 200 ml liquid
AMERICAN CUP
1 cup = 240 ml liquid (8 oz)
The recipes in this book were tested with the Indian teacup which holds 200 ml liquid.

Contents

Introduction   7

DRINKS   10

Minty Ambi Panna   11
Sardai   12
Lassi - Malai Maar Ke   12

Punjabi Kanji   13
Poodina Jeera Paani   13

SNACKS   14

Kele Aur Anjeer Ki Tikki   15
Lachhedar Dal Rolls   16
Saboodana Ka Mazaa   17
Bharwaan Palak Patte   18
Bhutte Ke Pakore   20
Gobhi Samosas   23
Paneer Tikka   24

Aloo Chaat   25
Vegetable Rolls   26
Punjabi Aloo Tikki   27
Phool Tukri   28
Paneer Pakore (Special)   29
Dahi Bhalle   30

CURRIES   31

Aloo Khus   32
Dhingri Matar   33
Angoori Gajar Kofte   34
Sarson da Saag   36
Punjabi Kadhi   37
Paneer Makhani   38
Pindi Chhole   41
Chitte Matar Tamatar   42

Punj Rattani Dal   43
Chana Arbi Naveli   44
Matar Khumba Curry   46
Punjabi Rajmah   47
Dal Makhani (Maanh Sabat)   48
Makai Vadi Chaska   49
Lahori Malai Kofte   50
Paalak Paneer   52

DRY & MASALA DISHES 53

Subziyaan Kali Mirch   54
Surkh Khumb   55
Til Mil Matar   56
Spinach Soya Keema   59
Dhania Patta Gobhi   60
Anjeeri Gobhi   62
Achaari Bhindi   63
Kamal Kakri Aur Singhara   64

Mirch Vadiyaa   65
Sukhi Urad ki Dal   66
Kathal Laajawaab   67
Gobi De Danthal   68
Sukhe Matar Aloo   69
Baingan Di Kachri   70
Gur Waale Shalgam   70

CHAAWAL 71

Matar Vadi Wale Chaawal   71
Aloo Gobhi Chaawal   72
Tikha Subzi Pulao   73

Achaari Chana Pulao   74
Kesar waala Pulao   77

ROTI 78

Poodina Parantha   78
Gur ka Parantha   79
Tandoori Roti   80
Makki di Roti   81

Amritsari Nan   81
Quick Peethi Poori   82
Bhature   82

ACHAAR & CHUTNEY 83

Instant Khatti Mithi Chutney   83
Amm Da Achaar   83
Dahi Poodina Chutney   84

Sirke Waale Pyaaz   84
Gobi Shalgam Da Achaar   85

MITHA (SWEETS) 86

Anjeeri Chenna Kulfi   86
Chana Dal & Khajur Halwa   87
Jalebi Te Rabri   88
Seb (apple) ka Meetha   89
Kesar waale Mitthe Chaawal   90

Chhuare Te Chaawal Di Kheer   91
Mithae Jauley   91
Coco Gulla   92
Anjeeri Halwa   92

 # DRINKS

Minty Ambi Panna

The sweet and sour Indian cooler prepared from raw mangoes.

Serves 6-8

½ kg raw green mangoes (kaccha aam)
a mint sprig (poodina)- for garnish

PASTE
½ cup mint leaves (poodina)
2 tsp roasted cumin (bhuna jeera) powder
¾ cup sugar
2 tsp salt

1. Peel raw mangoes. Discard skin.
2. Place peeled mangoes in a pressure cooker with 6 cups of water and pressure cook to give 2-3 whistles. Remove from heat.
3. When cool, extract the pulp of the mangoes with the hands and discard the seeds. Mix the pulp and water in the pressure cooker well.
4. Grind all the ingredients of a paste in a mixer by adding a little water to a smooth paste.
5. To the mango pulp, add the prepared mint paste. Mix well, till sugar dissolves.
6. Take a muslin cloth or a very fine metal strainer and strain the mixture. Check and adjust the seasonings as a lot depends on the sourness of the mangoes. Chill.
7. Pour the panna over ice put in glasses and garnish with a mint sprig.

Sardai

A healthy and refreshing milk drink.

Serves 2-3

250 ml (1¼ cups) milk
250 ml (1¼ cups) water
5 tbsp sugar or to taste

GRIND TOGETHER
10-15 almonds - soaked and peeled (blanched)
1½ tbsp khus khus (poppy seeds)
2 tsp magaz (melon seeds)
10 saboot kali mirch (peppercorns)
seeds of 2 chhoti illaichi (green cardamoms)

1. Soak almonds separately in warm water for 30 minutes. Peel and keep aside.
2. Soak together khus khus, magaz, kali mirch and chhoti illaichi for 30 minutes in some water.
3. Drain and grind the khus mixture along with the blanched almonds to a very fine paste, using a little water.
4. Add ½ cup water to the almond paste. Mix. Strain and squeeze well through a muslin cloth.
5. Add remaining (¾ cup) water and milk. Mix in the sugar. Serve chilled.

Lassi - Malai Maar Ke

Serves 1   *Picture on cover*

1 cup curd prepared from full cream buffalo milk
6-8 poodina (mint) leaves
½ cup water, salt and pepper to taste
½ tsp bhuna jeera powder (roasted & ground cumin seeds)

1. Beat or churn curd alongwith poodina very well, preferably in a mixer.
2. Add water, salt and pepper. Add ice and blend till frothy. Pour in a tall glass.
3. Sprinkle bhuna jeera powder and serve garnished with mint leaves.

Note: To prepare sweet lassi, add 2 tbsp sugar or gur (jaggery) to the churned curd instead of salt and pepper.

Punjabi Kanji

Red purple drink - The wine of Punjab.

Serves 12

½ kg fresh black carrots - peeled & cut into thin fingers
3 fully heaped tsp of rai powder
3 heaped tsp of salt, 2 pinches red chilli powder, ½ tsp kala namak (black salt)

1. Boil about 2 liters (8 cups, almost a patila full) water. When the water boils, remove pan from fire.
2. Add the carrots. Let them be in hot water for 4-5 minutes.
3. Add 2 more litres (8 more cups) of water and keep aside to cool. Let the water cool completely.
4. Add rai powder, salt, red chilli powder and kala namak. Mix well.
5. Transfer to an earthern or ceramic jar and keep in the sun for 2-3 days. Stir it every day.
6. After 2-3 days when it turns sour, it can be kept in the refrigerator and used as required. It is served chilled along with a few pieces of carrots.

Note: Rai powder should be added only after the water turns cold.

If black carrots are not available, ordinary carrots and 1 beetroot may be used.

Poodina Jeera Paani

Serves 4 *Picture on page 22*

4 cups water
1 rounded tbsp seedless tamarind (imli) or tamarind pulp
4 tsp lemon juice
1 tbsp sugar
½ tsp kala namak (black salt)
1½ tsp bhuna jeera (roasted cumin powder)
¾ tsp salt, or to taste
1 bunch of mint leaves & 1" piece ginger - ground to a paste
2 tbsp besan ki pakories or boondi (raite waali pakories)

1. Soak tamarind in 1 cup hot water. Extract pulp. Strain the pulp.
2. Grind poodina and ginger with a little water to a smooth paste.
3. Add poodina paste to tamarind water.
4. Add 3 more cups of water and all ingredients except pakories. Chill in the fridge.
5. To serve, pour in glasses filled with a little ice and sprinkle some pakories on top.

SNACKS

Tips...

- The most delicious snack in the world can fail to tempt if it is presented in an unbecoming manner! A greasy or too oily snack is no more appetizing, so make it a habit to remove the fried snack from oil on a tissue or a paper napkin to absorb the excess oil.

- A few crisp leaves of lettuce or a sprig of mint or coriander placed at the edge of the serving platter makes the snack irresistible! Make the green leaves crisp by putting them in a bowl of cold water and keeping them in the fridge for 3-4 hours or even overnight. Some cucumber slices or tomato wedges placed along with the greens, beautify it further.

- For getting a crisp coating on cutlets or rolls, dip prepared snack in a thin batter of maida and water and then roll in bread crumbs. Fry till well browned.

- A teaspoon of til (sesame seeds) or khus-khus (poppy seeds) or ajwain (carom seeds), added to coating mixture or bread crumbs makes the snack interesting.

- In the absence of bread crumbs, a mixture of ¼ cup maida and ½ cup suji may be used to get a crisp coating.

- If your cutlets fall apart, quickly tear 1-2 slices of bread and grind in a mixer to get fresh bread crumbs. Add it to the cutlet mixture for binding.

- To make crisp potato chips, soak them in cold water for 1 hour. Drain. Wipe dry and sprinkle some maida (plain flour) on them before frying.

- Never start frying in smoking hot oil as it will turn the snack black. Never fry in cold oil also as the snack may fall apart or it may soak a lot of oil.

- For deep frying any snack, add small quantities to the oil at one time. This maintains the oil's temperature. If too many pieces are added together, the oil turns cold and a lot of oil is then absorbed by the snack.

- After deep frying, let the oil cool down. Add a little quantity of fresh oil to the used oil before reusing. This prevents the oil from discolouring. Snacks...

Kele Aur Anjeer Ki Tikki

Makes 8   Picture on page 2

2 kache kale (raw bananas)
1 green chilli - finely chopped, ½" piece ginger - finely chopped
1 tbsp chopped coriander
1 tsp salt, ½ tsp garam masala, ½ tsp dhania powder

FILLING (GROUND TO A PASTE IN A MIXIE)
5- 6 anjeers (figs)
1 dry red chilli, 2 tbsp milk
TO COAT
3 tbsp maida or cornflour

1. Grind roughly chopped anjeer, dry red chilli to a paste in a mixer with 2 tbsp milk till smooth. Keep aside.

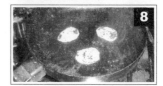

2. Cut 1 banana into ½. Peel half banana and cut into paper thin diagonal slices. If slices look big cut each diagonal slice further into 2 diagonal pieces. Sprinkle red chilli powder and salt. Mix well and keep aside.

3. Pressure cook the remaining 1½ bananas along with the peel (chilka) with 2 cups water to give 2 whistles. Remove from fire.

4. Peel boiled bananas. Grate the bananas (kelas) well. Add green chillies, finely chopped ginger, chopped coriander, salt, garam masala and dhania powder.

5. Take a small ball of banana mixture. Give a slight depression in the centre of the ball. Place about ¼ tsp - ½ tsp anjeer filling in the centre & cover well to form a ball again. Flatten ball to form a tikki (about 2"), such that the filling is completely covered on all sides with banana (kelas) mix. Flatten sides of the tikki also.

6. Roll the tikkis over cornflour spread in a plate.

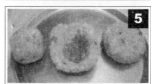

7. Heat oil on a tawa or a frying pan. Shallow fry 2-3 tikkis at a time in 2 tbsp oil in a non-stick pan till well browned and crisp on both sides. Repeat with all the tikkis. Remove tikkis from pan.

8. In the same pan , add 1 more tbsp of oil , add the kela (banana) slices. Pan fry till golden brown from both sides. Remove from pan.

9. Serve each tikki topped with a fried slice of kela.

Note: For a party you can deep fry the tikkis also.

Lachhedar Dal Rolls

An extremely crisp snack coated with thin vermicelli (long, thin, seviyaan).

Makes 12-14

2½ cups grated paneer (250 gms)
3 slices bread - churned in a mixer to get fresh bread crumbs
½ cup chopped coriander, ¾ tsp chaat masala
½ tsp bhuna jeera (roasted cumin), ¾ tsp salt, ½ tsp pepper

FILLING
¼ cup channa dal - soaked for 2 hours & ground coarsely without water in a mixer
1 onion - chopped finely
1 tsp ginger - chopped finely
1 tbsp kaju - chopped, 2 tbsp kishmish - chopped, 1 tbsp oil
¼ tsp haldi, ½ tsp salt, ¼ tsp red chilli powder, ¼ tsp amchoor, ½ tsp garam masala

TO COAT
½ cup very thin, long seviyaan- roughly broken into small pieces by hand

1. Strain dal and roughly grind in a mixer to a coarse thick paste. Do not grind too much and make it thin and smooth.
2. Heat oil. Add onion, ginger, kaju and kishmish. Cook till onions turn light golden.
3. Add ground dal, haldi, salt, red chilli powder, amchoor and garam masala. Stir for 1-2 minutes. Remove from fire and keep aside.
4. Mix grated paneer with coriander, chaat masala, fresh bread crumbs, bhuna jeera, salt and pepper.

5. With a ball of the paneer mixture, make a 2" long oval roll. Flatten it to get a slight depression in the centre. Place 1 tsp of the filling in it along the length. Pick up the sides to cover the filling, such that the filling is completely covered on all sides with the paneer mixture. Shape to give a neat roll with slightly flattened ends.

6. Break seviyaan into 1-1½" small pieces. Spread on a plate. Take 1 cup of water separately in a shallow flat bowl (katori). Dip the roll in the water for a second and then immediately roll it over the seviyaan. All the sides should be completely covered with seviyaan.
7. Keep aside to set for 15 minutes. Deep fry 2-3 pieces at a time. Serve with poodina chutney.

Saboodana Ka Mazaa

Serves 6

½ cup saboodana (sago) - soaked in 1 cup warm water for 1 hour
2 tsp khus khus (poppy seeds)
3 potatoes - boiled and grated
2 slices bread - tear into pieces and grind in a mixer to get fresh crumbs
1 tsp chopped ginger
1 green chilli- chopped
2 tbsp chopped green coriander
½ tsp garam masala
½ tsp red chilli powder
½ tsp amchoor, 1 tsp salt
½ cup roughly mashed paneer

TO FILL
1 tbsp thick malai
12 kishmish - soaked in water

1. Soak saboodana in about 1 cup warm water to cover it for ½-1 hour or till soft. Drain off excess water by putting in a strainer.
2. Mix grated boiled potatoes, fresh bread crumbs, khus-khus, ginger, green chilli, coriander, garam masala, red chilli powder, amchoor and salt.
3. Lastly mix in the mashed paneer gently. Shape into 12 balls.
4. Flatten each ball and place a drop of malai and 1 kishmish. Make a ball again and flatten to get oval pieces.
5. Press each piece on saboodana spread on a plate so that it sticks. Flatten some more. Deep fry 2-3 pieces in a kadhai at a time in medium hot oil till golden.

Bharwaan Palak Patte

Serves 4-5

24 spinach (paalak) leaves - with 2" long stems

FILLING
2 potatoes - boiled and grated
½ cup boiled or frozen peas - grind to a rough paste
2 tbsp oil
½ tsp jeera (cumin seeds)
½" piece ginger - chopped finely (1 tsp)
¼ tsp haldi
1 tsp salt, ¼ tsp garam masala, ¼ tsp chilli powder

BATTER
½ cup besan (gramflour)
¼ cup suji (semolina)
¾ cup water, approx.
½ tsp ajwain (carom seeds)
½ tsp salt

1. Break the spinach leaves along with a little stem, about 2" long. Wash and pat dry the leaves on a clean kitchen towel.
2. For filling, heat 2 tbsp oil. Add ½ tsp jeera and ginger. Wait for a minute.
3. Add ¼ tsp haldi. Stir to mix well.
4. Add paste of peas, salt, garam masala and red chilli powder. Cook for a minute.
5. Add grated potato and cook for 3-4 minutes. Remove from fire. Keep filling aside.
6. For the batter, mix all the given ingredients to get a batter of a coating consistency.
7. Place the spinach leaf flat on a plate with the right side up. Spread some filling on the leaf.
8. Place another leaf on it, keeping the wrong side outside.
9. Press well so that the two leaves stick together nicely.
10. At the time of serving, heat 4 tbsp oil in a pan. Keep aside.
11. Dip the spinach leaf in batter, coating it well with batter.
12. Deep fry the stuffed leaf till crisp on both sides. Remove on paper napkin.
13. Serve hot with chutney or tomato ketchup.

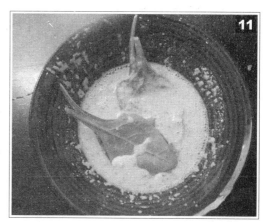

Finished Recipe

Bhutte Ke Pakore

Serves 6-8

3 large soft bhuttas or fresh corns (corn on cobs)
1¼ tbsp besan (gram flour)
2 tbsp chopped green coriander
1 green chilli - chopped
1 tsp salt or to taste, ¼ tsp pepper, oil for frying

MIXED CHUTNEY TO SERVE
¼ cup imli chutney
¼ cup poodina chutney

1. Grate the corn on the cobs (bhutta).
2. Add besan, coriander and chopped green chilli to the grated corn. Mix well. Keep aside.
3. At serving time, add salt and pepper to the corn mixture, mix well. Heat oil for frying.
4. Drop 1 tbsp of batter in medium hot oil, with the help of a spoon. (See picture).
5. Fry 4-5 pieces at a time on medium heat, till golden brown on all sides.
6. Drain on a paper napkin.
7. Mix both chutneys to get a spicy sauce. Dot each pakore with the mixed chutney.

Matar Khumba Curry: Recipe on page 46 ➤

Gobhi Samosas

Serves 8-10   *Picture on opposite page*

DOUGH
¾ cup plain flour (maida), ¼ cup fine semolina (suji)
¼ tsp salt, a pinch of baking powder
2 tbsp ghee or butter or margarine

VEGETABLE FILLING
1 medium cauliflower - grated (2 cups)
1 boiled potato - mashed coarsely (½ cup)
½" piece fresh ginger - grated
salt to taste, ½ tsp red chilli powder
1 tsp roasted, ground cumin seeds (bhuna jeera)
¼ tsp amchoor
1 tbsp each of cashews (kaju) and raisins (kishmish) - chopped
2 green chillies - deseeded and finely chopped, ¼ tsp sugar

1. Sift flour, semolina, salt and baking powder into a bowl. Rub in ghee or butter. Add a few tablespoons of cold water to form a firm dough. Knead for 5-7 minutes until the dough becomes smooth and elastic. Cover the dough and keep aside for 30 minutes or longer while making the filling.

2. To prepare filling, heat 3 tbsp oil in a pan. Remove from heat. Add ginger, salt, red chilli powder, bhuna jeera and amchoor.

3. Return to heat. Add kaju and kishmish. Cook for a few seconds. Add potatoes. Stir for a few seconds. Add cauliflower. Mix well. Add sugar and green chillies.

4. Cover and cook on low heat till the cauliflower is cooked. Make the filling spicy if you like. Keep aside.

5. Make lemon sized balls of dough. Roll out into thin rounds. Cut each circle in half. Brush some water on straight edges. Pick up the half circle & form a cone shape, overlapping straight edges ¼ inch & pressing firmly to seal the seam. Fill cone two-thirds with filling, about 1 tbsp of the filling in each cone.

6. Press together to make a secure joint.

7. Deep fry 8-10 pieces on low medium heat till golden. Drain on paper and serve with chutney.

TIP: Never fry the samosas on high heat and fry 8-10 pieces together in a single batch. If the oil is too hot, the outer covering gets browned very fast, without getting cooked properly.

◁ *Gobhi Samosas, Poodina Jeera Paani: Recipe on page 13*

Paneer Tikka

Serves 3-4

300 gm paneer - cut into 1½" squares of 1" thickness
1 large capsicum - deseeded and cut into 1" pieces (12 pieces)
1 onion - cut into 4 pieces and then separated

MARINADE
½ cup dahi- hang in a muslin cloth for 15 minutes
3 tbsp thick malai or thick cream
a few drops of orange colour or a pinch of haldi (turmeric)
1½ tbsp oil, 1 tbsp maida
½ tsp amchoor, ½ tsp kala namak, ¾ tsp salt, or to taste, 1 tbsp tandoori masala

GRIND TOGETHER
1" piece ginger, 5-6 flakes garlic
2 dried, whole red chillies - soaked in water for 10 minutes and drained

1. Hang curd in a muslin cloth for 15 minutes.
2. Drain soaked red chillies. Grind ginger, garlic and red chillies to a paste.

3. To the ginger-garlic-chilli paste, add hung dahi, cream or malai, colour or haldi, oil, 1 tbsp maida, amchoor, kala namak, salt, tandoori masala. Add paneer. Mix well.
4. Brush wire rack (grill) of the oven generously with oil.
5. Arrange paneer on a greased wire rack of the oven or on the skewers. After all the paneer pieces are done, put the capsicum and onions - both together in the left over marinade and mix well to coat the vegetables with the marinade. Leave the vegetables in the bowl itself.

6. At serving time, put the paneer pieces placed on the wire rack in the hot oven at about 200°C. Grill till almost done, for about 15 minutes. Grill the paneer till it gets dry and starts getting crisp. Sprinkle some oil on the paneer pieces. Now remove the vegetables from the bowl and put them also in the oven on the sides of the paneer. Grill everything together for another 5 minutes. The vegetables should not be grilled for too long.

7. Remove from the oven. Serve immediately (really hot), sprinkled with some lemon juice and chaat masala.

Aloo Chaat

Serves 6

4-5 boiled potatoes of medium size
1½ cups of boiled peas
1" piece of ginger - chopped fine
2-3 green chillies
1 tbsp chaat masala (prepare as given below and store the excess)
juice of ½ lemon
5-6 tbsp oil
salt to taste

CHAAT MASALA
¼ cup slightly roasted saboot dhania (coriander seeds)
¼ cup amchoor (dried mango powder)
¼ cup red chilli powder
¼ cup roasted jeera (cumin seeds)
¼ cup salt
¼ tbsp kala namak (rock salt)
½ tbsp saboot kali mirch (pepper corns)

1. Peel and cut boiled potatoes into 1" pieces.
2. Shallow fry the potato pieces in a frying pan in 5-6 tbsp oil till slightly brown in colour.
3. Remove the potatoes from oil. Keep potatoes aside.
4. For chaat masala, grind all the ingredients written under chaat masala to a smooth powder.
5. Heat only 1 tbsp of oil in the pan and fry ginger for 1 minute.
6. Add peas and fry for 1 minute. Remove from fire.
7. Add potatoes, peas, ginger, green chillies, chaat masala and lemon juice. Mix well. Add more salt if required.
8. Transfer to a serving bowl and garnish with fresh coriander leaves. Serve.

Vegetable Rolls

Serves 8

2 potatoes - chopped
¾ of a small cauliflower - cut into small florets
2 onions - chopped
1 cup boiled or frozen shelled peas
4 slices of bread - broken into pieces and ground in a mixer to get fresh crumbs
1" piece ginger and 5-6 flakes garlic - ground to a paste (2 tsp)
½ tsp red chilli powder, ½ tsp garam masala, 1½ tsp salt or to taste
2 tsp tomato sauce
1 green chilli - finely chopped
2 tbsp chopped fresh poodina
4-5 tbsp peanuts - crushed on a chakla-belan or ground to a coarse powder in a small spice grinder
1-2 drops kewra essence, 4 tbsp cornflour

FILLING
2 onions - sliced and deep fried till golden brown
5-6 tbsp very finely chopped poodina (mint)
1-2 drops of kewra essence
1 tbsp kishmish - soaked in water
4 tbsp thick malai
¼ tsp salt

1. Pressure cook potatoes, cauliflower, onion and peas with 1 cup water to give one whistle. Keep on low flame for 5 minutes. Remove from fire. Cool. Drain and leave in a sieve (channi) for about 5 minutes to remove excess moisture.
2. Return the vegetables to the cooker. Mash the vegetables with a potato masher and keep on fire for 2 minutes to dry completely. Remove from fire.
3. Add ginger- garlic, red chilli powder, garam masala, salt and tomato sauce to the mashed vegetables.
4. Also add green chilli, poodina, peanuts, cornflour and fresh bread crumbs to the mashed vegetables. Add essence and mix again. Keep aside.
5. Roughly tear the poodina leaves into small pieces. (Cutting reduces the fragrance of herbs).
6. For filling, mix all ingredients together. Keep aside.
7. Break off balls of the vegetable mixture and pat them into flat oval shapes about ½" thick.
8. Place a row of filling along the length. Pick up the sides to cover the filling and shape into rolls. Deep fry till golden.

Punjabi Aloo Tikki

Makes 10

½ kg (6 medium) potatoes - boiled and mashed
2 tbsp cornflour
1 tsp salt
ghee or oil for shallow frying

FILLING
1/3 cup channa dal (Bengal gram)
½ tsp jeera (cumin seeds)
2 green chillies - finely chopped
½" piece ginger - finely chopped
½ tsp red chilli powder
salt to taste
½ tsp chaat masala
½ tsp garam masala
1 tbsp coriander leaves - chopped

1. Soak channe ki dal for 3-4 hours.
2. Heat 1 tbsp oil or ghee in a kadhai. Add jeera, allow to splutter. Add chopped green chillies, chopped ginger, red chilli powder and salt.
3. Drain dal and add to the kadhai. Cover and let it cook on low heat till it turns soft and gets cooked. Sprinkle some water while it is being cooked.
4. Cook dal till soft and dry. Add chaat masala, garam masala and chopped coriander leaves. Remove from fire and keep aside to cool.
5. Boil, peel and mash potatoes. Add 2 tbsp cornflour and 1 tsp salt.
6. Grease the palm of your right hand. Take a ball of mashed potatoes on the oiled palm. Make a shallow cup with the ball of mashed potatoes.
7. Place a tbsp of dal filling in the centre and seal well to form a ball. Flatten the ball to form a tikki.
8. Heat oil on a tawa or a frying pan. Shallow fry 2-3 tikkis at a time till well browned and crisp on both sides.
9. Serve hot with imli and poodina chutney.

Final Recipe

Phool Tukri

Whole cauliflower/broccoli, batter fried and served in the tandoori style.

Picture on back cover   *Serves 4-5*

1 whole medium cauliflower or 1 whole broccoli flower

MARINADE
2 tbsp lemon juice, 1 tbsp ginger paste
1 tsp salt, ½ tsp red chilli powder
½ tsp ajwain (carom seeds)

BATTER
½ cup besan (gram flour)
¼ cup milk, approx.
1 tsp ginger paste, ½ tsp ajwain (carom seeds)
1 tbsp chopped coriander
½ tsp salt, ¼ tsp red chilli powder, ¼ tsp garam masala

TO SERVE
some onion rings, some chaat masala to sprinkle

1. Leaving 1" of the stem of broccoli/cauliflower, cut the rest of the stem. Boil 8 cups water with 2 tsp salt and 1 tsp sugar. Put the whole broccoli/cauliflower in it. Put the broccoli/cauliflower with stem side down. See that the whole broccoli/cauliflower is dipped in water. Bring to a boil again. Boil for 2-3 minutes till the stalk of the flower turn a little soft. Check with a knife. Remove from fire. Remove from water and refresh in cold water. Wipe dry with a clean kitchen towel.

2. Mix all ingredients of the marinade. Spread the marinade in-between the florets of the broccoli/cauliflower, especially from the backside. Keep aside for 15 minutes.

3. Mix all ingredients of the batter in a deep big bowl. Add enough milk to get a thick coating batter.

4. Heat oil for deep frying in a kadhai. Dip the broccoli/cauliflower in the batter. Spread the left over batter nicely with the hands on the broccoli/cauliflower to cover nicely.

5. Carefully put in medium hot oil and deep fry till light golden on medium heat. Reduce heat and fry on low heat till a little brown. Remove from fire. Cut into 4 pieces lengthwise with a long sharp knife, then further cut each piece into 2 (now you get 8 pieces).

6. Sprinkle some chaat masala on the broccoli/cauliflower. Serve immediately on a bed of onion rings sprinkled with some chaat masala.

Paneer Pakore (*Special*)

Serves 4

250 gm paneer, some chaat masala to sprinkle

FILLING
½ tsp ajwain (carom seeds)
1 small onion - grated and squeezed well
1" ginger piece - grated and crushed to a paste
3-4 flakes garlic - crushed
½ tsp chilli powder, ½ tsp garam masala
½ tsp salt, 1 tsp dhania powder, 1 tsp amchoor

BATTER
1 cup besan
1/3 cup water - approx.,
2 pinches baking powder
¾ tsp each red chilli powder and salt, or to taste
2 tbsp chopped coriander

1. Cut paneer into 1½" squares which are slightly thicker than ¼" thickness.
2. Slit the pieces of paneer, a little more than halfway but not till the end.
3. Sprinkle some chaat masala on them on both sides.
4. To prepare the filling, mix all ingredients of the filling together.
5. With the help of the knife insert some filling in the paneer pieces. Press well.
6. Make a thick batter with all the ingredients. Beat well and keep aside for 10 minutes.
7. Dip the stuffed pieces of paneer in the batter and deep fry in hot oil till golden.
8. Serve hot sprinkled with chaat masala.

Paneer Pakore

Dahi Bhalle

Makes 15

1½ cups (250 gm) urad dal - washed
½" piece ginger - very finely chopped
2 green chillies - chopped
½ tsp salt
¼ tsp soda-bicarb (mitha soda)
½ tsp jeera (cumin seeds)
oil for frying

MIX TOGETHER
3 cups curds - beat well till smooth
½ tsp powdered sugar
½ tsp red chilli powder, salt to taste
1 tsp bhuna jeera powder
¼ tsp kala namak
15-20 kishmish (raisins) - soaked in water for 10 minutes
2 tbsp finely chopped coriander

1. Wash and soak dal in enough water to cover the dal.
2. Soak it for 3 hours. Drain water and grind with the minimum amount of water to a paste. Do not over grind.
3. Add finely chopped ginger, green chillies and salt.
4. Add soda and beat well for 4-5 minutes till the mixture turns whitish and frothy. Add 2-3 tbsp hot water while beating.
5. Heat oil. With wet hands, make bhalla with dal batter into 2" discs. Sprinkle some jeera seeds on it. Press lightly to stick the jeera and flatten the bhalla.
6. Deep fry 5-6 bhallas at a time in hot oil till they swell. Reduce heat to medium and turn the side. Fry on low medium heat till light golden. Drain from oil, keep aside.
7. Boil 6 cups water with 2 tsp salt. Remove from fire and add the bhallas. Soak in salted hot water for 5 minutes.
8. Press out water lightly and arrange bhallas in a flat dish.
9. Beat curd. Add all the ingredients to the curd. Pour curd on the arranged bhallas. Garnish with red chilli powder, chopped coriander and bhuna jeera powder. Serve with imli chutney and extra beaten curd.

Note: You can pour some hari chutney and some imli chutney also on the bhallas.

CURRIES

Aloo Khus

Potatoes coated with poppy seed masala.

Serves 4

2 potatoes
3 tbsp oil
½ tsp rai (mustard seeds), ¾ tsp kalonji (nigella)
a pinch of methi dana (fenugreek seeds)
1 tej patta (bay leaf)
2 onions - chopped
1 tsp ginger-garlic paste
½ tsp haldi, ½ tsp salt
¼ tsp red chilli powder
1 tsp dhania powder
½ tsp garam masala, 1 tsp lemon juice

GROUND TO A PASTE WITH A LITTLE WATER
4 tsp khus khus (poppy seeds)

1. Dice potatoes into 1" squares and boil in salted water for 5-7 minutes.
2. Heat 3 tbsp oil, add rai, kalonji and methi dana. Wait till methi dana turns golden.
3. Add tej patta and chopped onion. Cook till onions turn golden brown.
4. Remove from fire. Add ginger-garlic paste, haldi, salt, red chilli powder, dhania powder and garam masala. Cook for a minute.
5. Add boiled potatoes and mix well for 1-2 minutes.
6. Add khus-khus paste, cook for 2 minutes.
7. Add ½ cup water. Boil. Cook uncovered for a minute. Add lemon juice. Serve hot garnished with coriander.

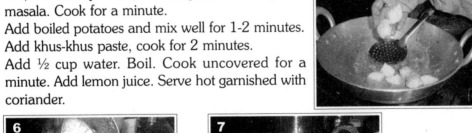

Dhingri Matar

Serves 4

Picture on page 57

1 cup shelled peas (matar)
25 gms dhingri (dry white mushrooms) - washed and soaked overnight
3 medium sized tomatoes
4 tbsp oil
4 laung (cloves), 1" stick dalchini (cinnamon)
some chopped coriander

GRIND TO A PASTE TOGETHER (ONION PASTE)
1 onion, 1" piece ginger, 6-7 flakes garlic
2 dry, red chillies (whole) - deseeded & soaked in water for 15 minutes
1 tsp salt, or to taste, ¼ tsp haldi powder (turmeric powder)

ROAST LIGHTLY ON A TAWA AND GRIND TO A POWDER
1 tbsp saboot dhania (coriander seeds)
1 tsp jeera (cumin seeds)
seeds of 2 moti illaichi (brown cardamoms)

1. Wash dhingri in 2-3 changes of water. Soak dhingri overnight. Next morning wash again in 3-4 changes of water. Cut dhingri into ½" pieces (small pieces) with a knife. Discard any very hard portion, if present.

2. Lightly roast on tawa - saboot dhania, jeera and moti illaichi seeds. Cool and powder finely.
3. Put tomatoes in boiling water, boil for 2-3 minutes. Remove the skin and puree.

4. Heat oil in a pan. Add laung and dalchini. Wait for a minute.
5. Add ground onion masala paste. Stir fry till onions turn brown and oil separates.
6. Add tomato puree. Cook till dry and oil separates.
7. Add dhingri to the fried masala and lower the heat and bhuno for 4-5 minutes.

8. Add peas and bhuno for another 1-2 minutes on low heat.
9. Add roasted powdered masala of jeera, dhania and moti illaichi. Mix.
10. Add enough water (about 1½ cups) to get a gravy. Boil and simmer covered till peas get cooked and oil separates. Serve hot.

Angoori Gajar Kofte

Picture on cover　　　　　　　　　*Serves 4*

KOFTAS (8 BALLS)
2 carrots - peeled & grated finely
1 potato - boiled and grated finely
1 green chilli - deseeded & chopped finely
a pinch of baking powder
½ tsp salt, or to taste, ¼ tsp red chilli powder, ¼ tsp amchoor, ¼ tsp garam masala
1 tbsp cornflour
1 tbsp chopped coriander

ONION PASTE (GRIND TOGETHER)
1 onion, 2-3 saboot kali mirch (black peppercorns)
1 moti illaichi (black cardamoms), 1-2 laung (cloves), 1" piece dalchini (cinnamon)

TOMATO PASTE (PUREE TOGETHER)
2 medium tomatoes, 1 tsp salt, or to taste, ¼ tsp red chilli powder
¼ tsp haldi powder, ½ tsp garam masala powder

OTHER INGREDIENTS
1½ tbsp besan (gram flour) - dry roast on a tawa
1 tej patta (bay leaves), ½ tsp ginger paste
1 tsp finely chopped or grated ginger
¼ cup milk
a few black or green grapes
2-3 tbsp cornflour to coat

1. Grate carrots finely from the finest side of the grater. Squeeze them.
2. Mix all ingredients given under koftas in a bowl. Knead the mixture well for 2-3 minutes till well blended. Check salt and masalas. Form into round - oval balls. Flatten a ball.
3. Place a grape. Shape into a ball or 1" long oval balls again. Spread 2-3 tbsp cornflour in a plate and roll the balls on it to coat. Dust off the excess flour.
4. Heat oil to deep fry the balls. Add only 2-3 balls at a time and carefully fry them on **medium flame** till they turn golden and get cooked from inside.
5. In the meanwhile, in another kadhai dry roast the besan till it turns light brown. Remove from fire and keep aside.
6. For gravy, heat 3 tbsp oil. Add 1 tej patta and onion paste & fry for 6- 7 minutes or till the paste turns brown
7. Add ginger paste and chopped ginger. Fry for a minute.
8. Add tomato paste. Cook on low heat for 8-10 minutes till dry and oil separates.
9. Add roasted besan. Mix well.

10. Add 1½ cups water. Boil. Simmer on low heat for 3-4 minutes. Remove from fire and let it cool down.

11. At serving time, add milk to the cold gravy and mix. Keep on fire and add the koftas and give 1-2 boils on low heat. Garnish with a few halved grapes. Serve.

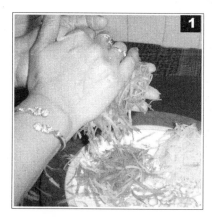

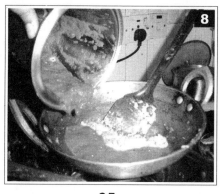

Sarson da Saag

Picture on page 76   *Serves 6*

1 bundle (1 kg) sarson (mustard greens)
250 gm paalak (spinach) or baathoo
2 shalgam (turnips) - peeled and chopped, optional
3-4 flakes garlic - finely chopped, optional
2" piece ginger - finely chopped
1 green chilli - chopped
¾ tsp salt, or to taste
2 tbsp makki ka atta (corn meal)
1½ tsp powdered gur (jaggery)

TADKA/TEMPERING
3 tbsp desi ghee
1" piece ginger - finely chopped
2 green chillies - finely chopped
½ tsp red chilli powder

1. Wash and clean mustard leaves. First remove the leaves and then peel the stems, starting from the lower end and chop them finely. (Peel stems the way you string green beans). The addition of stems to the saag makes it tastier but it is important to peel the stems from the lower ends. The upper tender portion may just be chopped. Chop the spinach or baathoo leaves and mix with sarson.
2. Put chopped greens with ½ cup water in a pan.
3. Chop garlic, ginger and green chilli very finely and add to the saag, add shalgam if you wish. Add salt and put it on fire and let it start heating.
4. The saag will start going down. Cover and let it cook on medium fire for 15-20 minutes. Remove from fire, cool.
5. Grind to a coarse paste. Do not grind too much and make it very smooth.
6. Add makki ka atta to the saag and cook for 15 minutes on low heat.
7. For tadka, heat desi ghee. Reduce heat and add ginger and green chillies. Cook till ginger changes colour. Remove from fire and add red chilli powder. Add ghee to the hot saag and mix lightly. Serve hot.
8. Serve with fresh home-made butter and makki-ki-roti.

Note: Fresh saag should have tender leaves and tender stems (gandal).

Punjabi Kadhi

Serves 4-6

1 small cup besan (gram flour)
2 cups khatti dahi (sour curd)
½ tsp haldi powder, 2½ tsp salt or to taste
¾ tsp red chilli powder (according to taste)

OTHER INGREDIENTS
2 tbsp oil
½ tsp jeera (cumin seeds), ½ tsp methi daana (fenugreek seeds)
1 moti illaichi (black cardamoms), 2 laung (cloves)
3-4 dry, red chillies

PAKORE (DUMPLINGS)
1 cup besan (gram flour), 1/3 cup water- approx.
1 big onion - chopped finely
1 small potato - chopped finely
½" piece ginger - chopped finely, 2 green chillies - chopped finely
½ tsp red chilli powder, 1 tsp salt, ½ tsp garam masala, 1 tsp dhania powder
a pinch of baking powder, oil for frying

TADKA/TEMPERING
2 tbsp oil, ½ tsp jeera (cumin seeds)
¼ tsp red chilli powder, preferably red chilli flakes

1. Mix khaati dahi, besan, salt, haldi, red chilli powder and 5½ cups water. Beat well till smooth and no lumps remain.
2. In a big heavy-bottomed pan, heat oil. Add jeera, methi daana, moti illaichi and laung. Add whole, red chillies too.
3. When jeera turns golden, add curd-water mixture. Stir continuously till it boils. After one good boil, lower heat and simmer for 15 minutes, stirring occasionally. Remove from fire and keep aside.
4. To prepare pakoras, mix besan with water to make a thick paste. Beat well. Add all other ingredients given under pakoras. Beat well to get a soft dropping batter.
5. Heat oil and drop spoonfuls of batter. Deep fry pakoras on medium heat till golden brown.
6. Add pakoras to the ready kadhi.
7. At serving time transfer the hot kadhi to a serving dish.
8. For the tadka, heat oil in small pan. Reduce flame and add jeera.
9. When it turns golden, remove from fire and red chilli. Pour oil on to the hot kadhi in the dish. Mix lightly. Serve hot with boiled rice.

Note: To get red chilli flakes, dry grind whole red chillies roughly in a small grinder.

Paneer Makhani

Picture on facing page   *Serves 4*

250 gm paneer - cut into 1" cubes
5 large (500 gm) tomatoes - each cut into 4 pieces
2 tbsp desi ghee or butter and 2 tbsp oil
4-5 flakes garlic and 1" piece ginger - ground to a paste (1½ tsp ginger-garlic paste)
1 tbsp kasoori methi (dry fenugreek leaves)
1 tsp tomato ketchup
½ tsp jeera (cumin seeds)
2 tsp dhania powder
½ tsp garam masala
1 tsp salt, or to taste
½ tsp red chilli powder, preferably degi mirch
½ cup water
½-1 cup milk, approx., ½ cup cream (optional)
3 tbsp cashewnuts (kaju)

1. Soak kaju in a little warm water for 10-15 minutes.
2. Drain kaju. Grind in a mixer to a very smooth paste using about 2 tbsp water.
3. Boil tomatoes in ½ cup water. Simmer for 4-5 minutes on low heat till tomatoes turn soft. Remove from fire and cool. Grind the tomatoes along with the water to a smooth puree.
4. Heat oil and ghee or butter in a kadhai. Reduce heat. Add jeera. When it turns golden, add ginger-garlic paste.
5. When paste starts to change colour add the above tomato puree & cook till dry.
6. Add kasoori methi and tomato ketchup.
7. Add masalas - dhania powder, garam masala, salt and red chilli powder. Mix well for a few seconds. Cook till oil separates.
8. Add cashew paste. Mix well for 2 minutes.
9. Add water. Boil. Simmer on low heat for 4-5 minutes. Reduce heat.
10. Add the paneer cubes. Remove from fire. Keep aside to cool for about 5 minutes.
11. Add enough milk to the cold paneer masala to get a thick curry, mix gently. (Remember to add milk only after the masala is no longer hot, to prevent the milk from curdling. After adding milk, heat curry on low heat.)
12. Heat on low heat, stirring continuously till just about to boil.
13. Add cream, keeping the heat very low and stirring continuously. Remove from fire immediately and transfer to a serving dish. Swirl 1 tbsp cream over the hot paneer in the dish. Serve immediately.

Sukhe Matar Aloo: Recipe on page 69, Paneer Makhani ➤

Pindi Chhole

Serves 4   *Picture on opposite page*

PRESSURE COOK TOGETHER
1 cup channa kabuli (Bengal gram)
2 tbsp channe ki dal (split gram)
2 moti illaichi (big cardamoms), 1" stick dalchini (cinnamon)
2 tsp tea leaves tied in a muslin cloth or 2 tea bags

MASALA
2 onions - chopped finely
1½ tsp anaardana (pomegranate seeds) powder
3 tomatoes - chopped finely
1" piece ginger - chopped finely
1 green chilli - chopped finely
1 tsp dhania powder, ½ tsp garam masala
½ tsp red chilli powder or to taste
1 tsp channa masala, 1¼ tsp salt or to taste

1. Soak channa & channe ki dal overnight or for 6-8 hours in a pressure cooker. Next morning, discard water. Wash channas with fresh water and add moti illaichi, dalchini, tea leaves, ¼ tsp soda and enough water to cover the channas nicely.
2. Pressure cook all the ingredients together to give one whistle. After the first whistle, keep on low flame for about 20-25 minutes. Keep aside.
3. Heat 4 tbsp oil. Add onions. Saute till transparent. Add anaardana powder. Cook stirring till onions turn golden brown. (Do not burn them).
4. Add chopped tomatoes, ginger and green chill. Stir fry for 3-4 minutes.
5. Add dhania powder, garam masala and chilli powder. Mash and stir fry tomatoes occasionally till they turn brownish in colour and oil separates.
6. Strain channas, reserving the liquid. Remove tea bag from the boiled channas.
7. Add the strained channas to the onion-tomato masala. Mix well.
8. Add salt. Stir fry gently for 5-7 minutes.
9. Add channa masala and salt. Add the channa liquid. Cook for 15-20 minutes on medium heat till slightly dry.

◁ Pindi Chhole, Bhature: Recipe on page 82

Chitte Matar Tamatar

Peas with tomatoes in a rich white gravy.

Serves 4

1 cup boiled or frozen peas
1 small firm tomato - cut into 8 pieces
2 tbsp cashewnuts (kaju) - soaked in ¼ cup hot water for 5 minutes
¾ cup dahi
seeds of 2 chhoti illaichi (green cardamoms)
3 tbsp oil
½ tsp jeera (cumin seeds)
2 tsp kasoori methi (dry fenugreek leaves)
1 tsp dhania powder, ½ tsp garam masala, ½ tsp red chilli powder
¼ tsp sugar, 1 tsp salt or to taste
½ cup milk
1 tsp tandoori masala

PASTE
2 onions, 1" piece ginger

1. Soak kaju in some water. Drain and grind along with curd and seeds of chhoti illaichi to a fine paste.
2. Heat 3 tbsp oil. Add jeera. Wait till it turns golden.
3. Add onion and ginger paste. Stir fry on low flame till light brown. Reduce flame.
4. Add kasoori methi, dhania powder, garam masala, red chilli, sugar and salt. Stir for ½ minute.
5. Gradually add curd-cashewnut mixture, a little at a time, stirring continuously. Bhuno for 4-5 minutes till masala turns thick and oil separates.
6. Add milk and 1 cup water. Boil stirring, on low heat. Simmer for 5-7 minutes, on low flame till gravy turns thick.
7. Add boiled peas. Mix.
8. Add tomato pieces and tandoori masala. Give 2-3 boils and serve hot.

Punj Rattani Dal

A combination of five lentils are used to prepare this dal delicacy.

Serves 4

5 DALS
(WASH ALL DALS AND SOAK TOGETHER FOR 2 HOURS)
¼ cup saboot moong dal (green)
¼ cup saboot masoor dal (brown)
¼ cup saboot urad dal (black)
¼ cup channa dal (yellow)
¼ cup arhar dal (yellow)

OTHER INGREDIENTS
2 tbsp ghee
1 tsp shah jeera (black cumin seeds)
½ onion - chopped
2 tsp dhania powder, ½ tsp red chilli powder
½ tsp haldi, 1½ tsp salt, or to taste

TEMPERING/TADKA
4 tbsp white or yellow butter
1 tomato - chopped finely
½ cup yoghurt (dahi) - beat well till smooth
½ tsp garam masala
seeds of 1 moti illaichi (black cardamom) - crushed on a chakla- belan
½ tsp red chilli powder
¼ cup coriander - chopped

1. Heat 2 tbsp ghee in a heavy bottomed pan. Add shah jeera and saute over medium heat until they begin to crackle.
2. Add chopped onion, saute until light brown.
3. Drain all the dals and add to the onion. Bhuno for 4-5 minutes on low heat.
4. Add about 5 cups water and bring to a boil. Reduce heat and remove scum.
5. Add dhania powder, red chilli powder, haldi and salt, cover and cook on low heat for about 30 minutes or until lentils are done.
6. To prepare the tadka, melt butter in a kadhai, add chopped tomatoes, yoghurt and garam masala, bhuno over medium heat, stirring until the fat leaves the sides. Add crushed seeds of moti illaichi. Stir for a few seconds. Add red chilli powder.

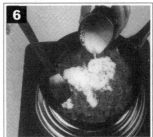

7. Add the cooked lentils and stir for 3-4 minutes. Remove to a bowl, garnish with coriander and serve hot.

Chana Arbi Naveli

Picture on page 58　　　　　　　　　　*Serves 4*

125 gm arbi (colocassia) of medium size
1 cup boiled kale chaane (black gram)
1½ tbsp besan (gram flour)
¼ tsp red chilli powder
¼ tsp salt or to taste

OTHER INGREDIENTS
1 tsp salt, ½ tsp red chilli powder, ½ tsp garam masala
1 tbsp mango chutney, home made or ready made
2 tomatoes - pureed in the mixer
3 tbsp curd - well beaten till smooth
½ cup milk

SOAK TOGETHER
1 tbsp khus-khus (poppy seeds) and 1 tbsp magaz (melon seeds) - soaked together
in ½ cup warm water for 15 minutes

GRIND TO A PASTE
2 onions
3- 4 flakes garlic, 1" piece ginger

1. Pressure cook whole arbi with 3 cups water and 1 tsp salt to give one whistle. Keep on low flame for 2-3 minutes. Remove from fire. Cool and drain.
2. Peel & slice each arbi into ¼" thick round slices. Sprinkle ¼ tsp salt & ¼ tsp red chilli powder on arbi slices. Sprinkle dry besan. Over turn the pieces & sprinkle salt, red chilli powder and besan on this side too. Mix, so as to coat lightly.
3. Heat oil in a kadhai. Deep fry arbi till well fried and crisp.
4. Soak magaz and khus-khus in ½ cup water for 15 minutes.
5. Drain khus and magaz. Grind it along with onions, garlic and ginger to a smooth paste. Check that the khus is finely ground. Keep onion paste aside.
6. Heat 4 tbsp oil in a kadhai and stir fry the prepared onion paste for 2-3 minutes.
7. Add pureed tomatoes, salt, red chill powder, garam masala and mango chutney. Cook for 3-4 minutes or till oil separates on medium heat, stirring in between.
8. Add kale chhane. Mix. Cook covered for about 5 minutes on low heat.
9. Reduce heat, add beaten curd, and cook uncovered for 2-3 minutes, stirring frequently in between. Cook till curd dries.
10. Add 1 cup water. Boil. Cook on low flame till it comes to a boil. Simmer on low heat for about 5 minutes till gravy is ready.

contd...

11. Reduce heat, add milk stirring continuously. Stir for 2 minutes on low heat. Add arbi and cook for a minute. Check salt. Remove from fire and serve hot, garnished with some chopped coriander.

Matar Khumba Curry

Picture on page 21   *Serves 6-8*

1 packet (200 gm) mushrooms (khumba) - trim stalks & cut into 4 pieces
1 cup peas (shelled), 4 tbsp oil
2 moti illaichi (black cardamoms)
2 laung (cloves)
2 tsp salt, or to taste
2 tsp dhania powder
¼ tsp each - red chilli powder, garam masala, haldi

GRIND TOGETHER TO A PUREE
3 tomatoes
1 green chilli

GRIND TOGETHER TO A PASTE
1 large onion
6-8 flakes garlic, 1" piece ginger

1. Trim the end of the stalk of each mushroom and cut each into 4 pieces.
2. Heat oil. Add moti illaichi and laung. Wait for 1 minute.
3. Add onion-garlic-ginger paste. Cook stirring continuously light till brown. Remove from fire.
4. Add masalas - salt, dhania powder, red chilli powder, garam masala and haldi.
5. Return to low heat and cook for a few seconds. Add 1 tbsp water.
6. Add the tomato-green chilli puree. Cook till dry and oil separates.
7. Add mushrooms and peas. Stir fry for 5 minutes. Add 1-2 tbsp water if required.
8. Add 2 cups water. Cook on low medium heat for about 15 minutes till peas turn soft and oil separates. Serve curry with rice or chappatis.

Punjabi Rajmah

Serves 6

1½ cups lal rajmah (red kidney beans) - soaked overnight
1 tbsp channe ki dal (split gram) - soaked overnight
2½ tsp salt or to taste
2 onions
1" piece ginger, 6-8 flakes garlic
5 tbsp oil
1 tej patta (bay leaf)
1 moti illaichi (black cardamom)
2 laung (cloves)
¼ tsp haldi, 3 tsp dhania powder, ¼ tsp amchoor
½ tsp garam masala, 1 tsp red chilli powder, or to taste
3 tomatoes - pureed in a blender
½ cup curd - beaten well
2 tbsp chopped coriander

1. Pressure cook rajmah, channe ki dal with salt together with about 10 cups water to give one whistle. Keep on low flame for 15 minutes. Remove from fire.
2. Grind onion, ginger and garlic to a paste.
3. Heat 5 tbsp oil in a heavy bottomed kadhai. Add tej patta, moti illaichi and laung. Wait for 1 minute.
4. Add onion paste and stir fry till golden brown.
5. Reduce heat. Add haldi, dhania powder, amchoor, garam masala and red chilli powder. Stir for a few seconds.

6. Add tomatoes pureed in a blender. Cook till tomatoes turn dry and oil separates.
7. Reduce heat. Add beaten curd and stir continuously on low flame till the masala turns red again and oil separates.

8. Strain and add the rajmahs, keeping the water aside. Stir fry on medium flame for 2-3 minutes, mashing occasionally.
9. Add the water of the rajmahs and pressure cook again for 8-10 minutes on low flame after the first whistle.
10. Remove from fire. Add freshly chopped coriander leaves. Serve hot with chappatis or boiled rice.

Dal Makhani *(Maanh Sabat)*

Picture on page 94   *Serves 6*

1 cup urad saboot (whole black beans)
2 tbsp rajmah (kidney beans) - soaked for at least 6 hours or overnight, optional
1 tbsp ghee or oil
5 cups of water, 1 ½ tsp salt
2 dry whole red chillies, preferably Kashmiri red chillies
1" piece ginger, 4 flakes garlic (optional)
3 tbsp ghee or oil
4 tomatoes - pureed in a grinder
½ tsp garam masala, 2 tsp dhania (coriander) powder
1 tbsp kasoori methi (dry fenugreek leaves)
2 tbsp butter
¼ cup fresh malai, beaten well and mixed with ¼ cup milk to make it ½ cup

1. Clean, wash dal. If you want to add rajmah, soak dal and rajmah together in a pressure cooker for 6 hours or overnight.
2. Grind ginger and garlic together to a paste.
3. Discard water from the soaked dal. Add 6 cups of fresh water.

4. Pressure cook dal and rajmah with 1 tbsp ghee, salt, half of the ginger-garlic paste and the dry, red chillies. Keep the left over paste aside.
5. After the first whistle, keep on low flame for 20 minutes. Remove from fire. After the pressure drops, mash the hot dal a little. Keep aside.

6. Heat 3 tbsp ghee. Add tomatoes pureed in a grinder. Cook until thick and dry.
7. Add the left over ginger-garlic paste, garam masala and coriander powder. Cook until ghee separates.
8. Add kasoori methi. Cook further for 1-2 minutes.
9. Add this tomato mixture to the boiled dal.
10. Add butter. Simmer on low flame for 30 minutes, stirring and mashing the dal occasionally with a kadchhi against the sides of the cooker.
11. Add beaten malai mixed with milk. Mix very well with a kadchhi. Simmer for 5 minutes more, to get the right colour and smoothness. Remove from fire.

Note: Originally the dal was cooked by leaving it overnight on the burning coal angithis. The longer the dal simmered, the better it tasted.

Makai Vadi Chaska

Serves 4 *Picture on page 2*

1 cup tinned corn
1 Amritsari vadi (dried lentil cake)
3 tbsp oil
1 tsp shah jeera (royal black cumin)
1 onion - chopped
½ tsp haldi, 1 tsp dhania powder
¼ tsp amchoor, 1 tsp salt, or to taste
½" piece ginger - chopped (1 tsp)
4 tomatoes - chopped

1. Heat 1 cup oil in a kadhai, add whole vadi and fry vadi, turning sides till well browned on both sides. Remove vadi on a paper napkin. Break vadi into very very small pieces. Remove oil also from the kadhai.
2. Heat 3 tbsp oil in the same kadhai, add shah jeera, wait for a minute.
3. Add the chopped onion. Stir fry on medium flame till golden.
4. Add haldi, dhania powder, amchoor and salt. Mix.
5. Add vadi. Stir till onion masala turns golden brown.
6. Add chopped tomatoes and ginger. Cook till they turn dry for about 20 minutes.
7. Add corn and 2½ cups water. Give one boil. Cook covered on low flame for another 10 minutes.
8. Reduce heat. Break the vadi into even more smaller pieces, with a spoon and cook covered for another 2 minutes. Serve hot .

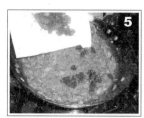

Note: Curry prepared with desi tomatoes tastes better than that made with the regular tomatoes.

Lahori Malai Kofte

Serves 6

150 gms paneer (cottage cheese) - grated
2 small boiled potatoes - grated
2 tbsp maida
½ tsp garam masala, ½ tsp red chilli powder, ¾ tsp salt, or to taste
2-3 tbsp maida (plain flour) - to coat

FILLING
½ onion - very finely chopped
½" tsp piece ginger - very finely chopped
4-5 kajus (cashews) - chopped
¼ tsp each of salt, red chilli powder, garam masala

GRAVY
a few strands kesar (saffron)
3 big onions, 1½" piece ginger, 2 dry, red chillies
2 tej patta (bay leaf), 4-5 chhoti illaichi (green cardamoms)
4 tbsp kaju (cashewnuts) - powdered
½ cup fresh thin malai - beaten with a fork or churned in the mixie for a second
3 tbsp desi ghee
½ tsp garam masala, ¾ tsp red chilli powder, 1½ tsp salt, or to taste
1 tbsp kasoori methi
1½ cups milk mixed with 2 cups water

1. To prepare the koftas, mix grated paneer, potatoes, red chilli powder, salt, garam masala and 2 tbsp maida.
2. Mix well till the mixture is smooth. Make 12 balls.
3. For the filling, heat 2 tsp ghee. Add onions and ginger. Fry till golden brown. Add kaju, salt, garam masala and chilli powder. Remove from fire.
4. Flatten each ball of paneer mixture, put 1 tsp of onion filling in each ball. Form a ball again. Roll each ball in maida. Dust to remove excess maida.

5. Deep fry 1-2 koftas at a time in medium hot oil. Keep aside.
6. To prepare the gravy, soak kesar in 1 tbsp warm water.
7. Grind onions, ginger and dry red chillies to a fine paste.

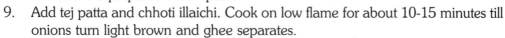

8. Heat 2 tbsp ghee in a heavy bottomed kadhai and add the prepared onion paste.
9. Add tej patta and chhoti illaichi. Cook on low flame for about 10-15 minutes till onions turn light brown and ghee separates.
10. Add masalas - garam masala, red chilli powder and salt.
11. Add malai. Cook for 3-4 minutes till masala turns brown again.
12. Add kaju powder. Cook for ½ minute.
13. Add milk mixed with water, to make a gravy. Boil. Simmer on low flame for 5 minutes.
14. Add kasoori methi. Discard bay leaves from the gravy.
15. Add kesar soaked in water, keeping aside a little for garnishing.
16. To serve, boil gravy. Add koftas. Keep on low heat for ½ a minute. Serve immediately, sprinkled with cream and dotted with soaked kesar.

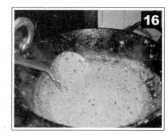

Final Recipe

Paalak Paneer

Serves 4

200 gm paneer - cut into 1" pieces and deep fried till golden brown
500 gm paalak (spinach) - chopped (5 cups)
3-4 green chillies - chopped
4 tbsp desi ghee or oil
6 tbsp ready-made tomato puree or 2 medium sized tomatoes - pureed in a mixie
1 tsp salt, or to taste, ½ tsp haldi powder, 1 tsp garam masala
1 laung and 1 chhoti illaichi - crushed, ½ cup milk

PASTE
2 big onions, 2" piece ginger, 10-12 flakes garlic (optional)

TADKA
1-2 tbsp ghee or oil, 1 tsp red chilli powder
1" piece ginger - finely chopped
1-2 green chillies - cut into 2 pieces

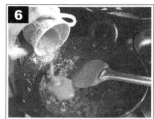

1. Cut paneer into 1" pieces and deep fry till golden.
2. Discard stems of palak leaves. Wash leaves in lots of water to remove grains of sand or soil.
3. Pressure cook palak with ¼ cup water to give one whistle. Keep on low flame for 5 minutes. Remove from fire. Cool.
4. Grind cooked paalak along with green chillies in a mixie to a coarse paste.
5. Heat ghee, add onion- garlic paste. Cook till onion turn golden.
6. Add tomato puree and cook on low flame for 2 minutes.
7. Add salt, haldi and garam masala. Stir for 1 minute.
9. Add paalak and cook for 2 minutes. Add crushed laung and chhoti illaichi.
10. Add 1½ cups hot water to make it thinner. Boil. Keep on low flame for 10-15 minutes. Add milk and cook for another 2 minutes. Remove from fire & transfer to a serving dish.
11. At serving time, heat ghee for tadka. Add ginger. Cook on low heat till it turns golden. Remove from fire and add green chillies. Mix. Add red chilli powder and immediately pour over the hot palak. Serve.

  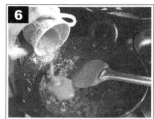

DRY & MASALA DISHES

Step 1, 2 of Subziyaan Kali Mirch

Subziyaan Kali Mirch

Picture on page 4   *Serves 5-6*

3-4 tbsp butter (preferably Amul)
2 tbsp grated ginger
1 onion- sliced, 1 tsp salt, or to taste
1¼ tsp freshly ground pepper (grind or crush few saboot kali mirch coarsely in a
spice grinder or on a chakla belan)
2-3 tbsp thick cream

VEGETABLES
1 potato - cut into 1" pieces and deep fried
100 gms paneer- cut into small (about ½") square pieces
1 green capsicum - deseed and cut into thin fingers
1 long, firm tomato - cut into 4 and then cut into thin long pieces
5-6 French beans - cut into ¼" pieces (½ cup)
1 carrot - cut into round slices
1 tbsp lemon juice (adjust to taste)

GARNISHING
some chopped coriander, 1-2 saboot kali mirch (peppercorns) - crushed

1. Cut tomato and capsicum into thin fingers.
2. Chop french beans into ¼" pieces. Cut potato into 1" pieces. Cut carrots into round slices.
3. Boil 2 cups water with ¾ tsp salt and ½ tsp sugar. Add carrots and beans after the water boils. Boil for just 1-2 minutes till crisp-tender. Refresh in cold water. Strain. Keep aside.
4. Deep fry potatoes in a kadhai to a golden brown colour on medium heat and check that they get cooked on frying.
5. Heat butter on medium flame. (If the heat is too much, the butter will burn). Add grated ginger. Fry on medium heat till slightly brown.
6. Add onions. Stir till golden.
7. Add beans, carrot, salt and pepper. Stir fry for 2 minutes.
8. Lower heat, add tomatoes. Cook covered for 2 minutes.
9. Add capsicum, paneer, fried potatoes and cream. Mix and remove from fire. Add lemon juice to taste. Serve sprinkled with pepper.

Surkh Khumb

A hot and bright red coloured, dry mushroom dish.

Serves 4

1 packet mushrooms (200 gms) - cut each into 2 pieces
1 tbsp butter or oil
3 tbsp oil/ghee
¼ tsp ajwain (carom seeds)
2 tomatoes - finely chopped
¾ tsp dhania powder, 1 tsp salt, ¼ cup mint leaves (poodina) - keep whole
½ cup milk

GRIND TOGETHER
3 dry, whole red chillies - deseeded and soaked in water for 10 minutes
2 medium sized onion
8-10 flakes garlic, 1" piece ginger

1. Trim the stem of each mushroom. Cut them into 2 pieces.
2. Heat 1 tbsp butter or oil in a kadhai and add the mushrooms. Stir fry on high flame till dry and golden. Add a pinch of salt, mix well. Keep aside.
3. Heat 3 tbsp oil or ghee. Add ajwain, wait for a minute.
4. Add ground red chilli- onion paste. Fry well for about 3-4 minutes or till the onion masala leaves oil.
5. Add tomatoes and fry for 2-3 minutes or till the tomatoes turn pulpy and get well mixed.
6. Add dhania powder and salt. Mix. Stir fry for a minute.
7. Add whole poodina leaves and fried mushrooms. Mix well.
8. Reduce heat, add milk, stirring. Cook for a minute. Serve.

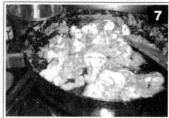

Til Mil Matar

Picture on page 1   *Serves 4*

2 cups shelled peas (matar) - boiled
1 tomato - cut into 8 pieces
2 tbsp dried fenugreek leaves (kasoori methi)
2 tbsp oil
1¼ tsp sesame seeds - dry roasted, to garnish

SPICE MIXTURE
(GRIND TOGETHER WITH A FEW TBSP OF WATER)
2 onions - roughly chopped
2 flakes garlic
2 tsp sesame seeds (til)
1 tsp cumin seeds (jeera)
1 tsp ground coriander (dhania powder)
½ tsp red chilli powder
¼ tsp turmeric (haldi), 1 tsp salt, or to taste

1. To prepare the spice mixture, grind onion, garlic, sesame seeds, cumin seeds, coriander powder, red chilli powder, haldi and salt with a little water to a fine paste in a coffee or spice grinder.
2. Heat 2 tbsp oil in a pan or a wok. Reduce heat. Add the spice mixture and fry for about 2 minutes, stirring continuously.
3. Add tomato pieces, boiled peas and kasoori methi. Stir fry for 4-5 minutes on low heat.
4. Serve sprinkled with a few roasted sesame seeds (til).

Dhingri Matar : Recipe on page 33 ➤

Spinach Soya Keema

Serves 4

1½ cups soya nutri granules - soak together for 15 minutes
2 cups milk
3 cups shredded spinach (paalak)
(125 gm) 8 mushrooms - grated (2 cups)
2 tbsp oil
3-4 flakes garlic - crushed, 2-3 dry, red chillies
1 tsp jeera
2 onions - chopped, 1 tsp finely chopped ginger
1½ cups soya granules - soak together for 15 minutes
¼ tsp haldi, 1 tsp dhania powder (coriander powder)
½ tsp red chilli powder, 1 tsp salt, ¼ tsp garam masala
1 tbsp lemon juice
seeds of 3 chhoti illaichi - crushed

1. Shred spinach into thin long pieces. Measure 3 cups of shredded spinach. Wash in several changes of water. Keep aside.
2. Soak soya granules in milk. Keep aside for 15-20 minutes.
3. Crush garlic and dry red chillies together in a small spice grinder.
4. Heat 2 tbsp oil in a pan. Add 1 tsp jeera. Wait for a few seconds.
5. Add crushed garlic and dry red chillies. Mix and cook till garlic turns golden.
6. Add onion, cook till golden brown. Add chopped ginger. Stir.
7. Add grated mushrooms and cook for 2-3 minutes, stirring on high flame.
8. Add paalak, mix well for 2 minutes on high flame, stirring.
9. Add soaked granules.
10. Add haldi, dhania powder, red chilli powder, salt and garam masala. Bhuno for 7-8 minutes till dry and oil separates.
11. Add lemon juice and powdered chhoti illaichi. Mix well and serve hot.

⊰ Chana Arbi Naveli : Recipe on page 44

Dhania Patta Gobhi

A delicious dry cabbage dish with a strong dhania (coriander) flavour, as both dry and fresh dhania is used in it preparation.

Serves 4-5

½ kg cabbage (1 medium flower) - cut into 1" square pieces
2 medium potatoes - peeled and cut into 8 pieces
3-4 tbsp oil/ghee
2 tsp ginger-garlic paste or paste of 1" piece ginger & 5-6 flakes garlic
2 tbsp dhania powder
½ cup ready made tomato puree
¼ cup dahi - beat well till smooth
1 tsp salt, or to taste
¼ tsp red chilli powder
½ tsp garam masala powder
2 tbsp mango chutney (ready made or home made)
¼ cup chopped hara dhania (fresh coriander)

1. Cut cabbage into 1" square pieces.
2. Peel potatoes and cut into 1" square pieces.
3. Heat oil/ghee in a kadhai. Reduce flame and add garlic and ginger paste. Fry till light brown.
4. Add dhania powder. Fry for 1 minute on low heat.
5. Add potato pieces, cook covered on low heat for 5 minutes. Sprinkle some water inbetween and cook covered till potatoes turn tender.
6. Add tomato puree, cook covered for 2 minutes.
7. Reduce heat, add well beaten dahi and cook for a minute, stirring constantly.
8. Add cabbage, salt, red chilli powder, garam masala and mango chutney.
9. Lower heat, and cook uncovered, stirring occasionally, for about 10 minutes till the cabbage is cooked.
10. Add lots of fresh green coriander. Mix well and remove from fire. Serve.

Steps of Dhania Patta Gobhi

Anjeeri Gobhi

Fried cauliflower, cooked in an anjeer flavoured masala. Something new, try it!

Picture on page 75   *Serves 6*

1 medium cauliflower (gobhi) - cut into medium size florets with long stalks
1 tsp jeera (cumin seeds)
2 onions - chopped
¾" piece ginger- chopped (2 tsp)
5 flakes garlic - chopped
2 green chillies - deseeded & chopped

ANJEER PASTE
8 small anjeers (figs)
1 cup dahi (yogurt)
1 tsp garam masala, ¾ tsp red chilli powder
1¾ tsp salt or to taste

TO SPRINKLE
2 small anjeers (figs) - chopped and roasted on a tawa (griddle)

1. Break the cauliflower into medium florets, keeping the stalk intact.
2. Heat 1 cup oil in a kadhai. Add all the cauliflower pieces and fry to a golden colour. Remove from oil and keep aside.
3. Churn all the ingredients given under anjeer paste in a mixer till smooth.
4. For masala, heat 2 tbsp oil in a kadhai. Add jeera. When it turns golden, add chopped onions. Stir till light brown.
5. Add chopped ginger, garlic and green chillies. Cook for a minute.
6. Add the prepared anjeer paste. Stir-fry for 2-3 minutes till the curd dries up a little. Keep aside till serving time.
7. Chop finely 2 anjeers and roast on a tawa till fragrant. Keep aside.
8. At serving time, heat the masala and add fried cauliflower. Mix well.
   Serve hot, sprinkled with roasted pieces of anjeer.

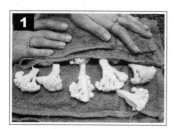

Achaari Bhindi

An unusual combination of bhindi in a masala, flavoured with pickle spices.

Serves 4   *Picture on page 75*

½ kg bhindi (lady's finger)
4 big (300 gms) tomatoes - chopped finely
2 tsp ginger or garlic paste
15-20 curry leaves
½ tsp haldi
½ tsp red chilli powder, 1 tsp dhania powder
¾ tsp salt, or to taste

ACHAARI SPICES
a pinch of hing (asafoetida)
1 tsp saunf (fennel), ½ tsp rai (mustard seeds)
½ tsp kalonji (onion seeds)
¼ tsp methi daana (fenugreek seeds)

1. Wash bhindi and wipe dry. Cut the tip of the head of each bhindi, leaving the pointed end as it is. Now cut the bhindi vertically from the middle making 2 smaller pieces from each bhindi.
2. Heat oil in a kadhai and deep fry the bhindi on medium heat in 2 batches. Do not over fry the bhindi, it should retain it's green colour. Drain on a paper napkin. Keep aside.
3. Heat 2 tbsp oil and add ginger or garlic paste. Add curry patta and stir fry for a minute.
4. Add achaari spices. Stir till methi daana turns brown.
5. Add haldi, chilli powder, dhania powder and salt. Stir for 30 seconds.
6. Add chopped tomatoes and stir for about 7-8 minutes or till oil separates.
7. Add fried bhindi. Sprinkle ¼ tsp salt and stir gently on slow fire for a few minutes till well mixed. Serve hot.

Kamal Kakri Aur Singhara

Picture on page 94   *Serves 4*

300 gm (2 medium) bhein or kamal kakri (lotus stem), thick ones
1 cup very finely shredded/ sliced spinach
3- 4 singahras - peeled and sliced (see note)
3 tbsp saunf- powdered in a mixie
4 tbsp desi ghee or oil
1 tsp jeera (cumin seeds)
2 onions - chopped
1 tsp chopped ginger
1 tsp chopped garlic
1 green chilli - chopped
¾ tsp salt or to taste, ½ tsp red chilli powder
½ tsp haldi (turmeric powder)
½ tsp amchoor, 1 tsp dhania powder
½ tsp garam masala
3 tbsp besan
¼ cup milk

1. Peel bhein. Cut diagonally into 1½" long thin pieces.
2. Put bhein in a pressure cooker with 1 cup water and ½ tsp salt. Keep on fire to give 2 whistle and then reduce heat and keep for 15 minutes on low heat. Remove from fire and pat dry gently on a paper napkin. Sprinkle some orange colour on the slices. Mix gently to get colour on all the slices.
3. Heat oil in a karahi and deep fry the bhein slices till golden. Keep aside.
4. Heat 4 tbsp oil in a large kadhai. Add jeera wait for a minute.
5. Add onion and cook till golden brown.
6. Add powdered saunf, ginger, garlic, chopped green chilli, salt, red chilli powder, haldi, amchoor, dhania powder and garam masala. Cook for 2 minutes.
7. Add spinach and cook for 3- 4 minutes.
8. Add besan and bhuno for 2 minute on low heat.
9. Add the bhein and singhara. Stir fry for 3- 4 minutes on medium flame till well browned.
10. Reduce heat, add milk and cook for 4- 5 minutes. Mix well. Serve hot.

Note: You can use 1 small potato cut into thin slices instead of singharas.

Mirch Vadiyaa

Capsicums and crisp golden potatoes with a wonderful spice blend.

Serves 4-5

3-4 capsicums - cut into 8-12 pieces (1" pieces)
2 tomatoes - cut into 8 pieces (1" cubes)
2 potatoes - boiled & each cut into 8 pieces (1" pieces)
juice of 1 lemon (2 tbsp)
3 tbsp oil
½ tsp jeera (cumin seeds)
1" piece ginger - chopped
¼ tsp haldi, 1 tsp salt, or to taste

FLAVOURFUL MASALA
seeds of 3 chhoti illaichi (green cardamoms)
2-3 laung (cloves)
seeds of 2 moti illaichi (black cardamom)
1" stick dalchini (cinnamon)

1. Cut capsicum and tomato into 1" pieces.
2. Boil potatoes, peel and cut into 1" pieces.
3. Crush all ingredients of the flavourful masala to a rough powder.
4. Heat oil in a kadhai/pan. Add jeera. Let it turn golden.
5. Add ginger. Add haldi.
6. Add potatoes and bhuno for 5-6 minutes till crisp and golden. Keep the potatoes spread out in the kadhai. Do not overlap them and do not stir too often. Let them turn crisp.
7. Add capsicum and tomatoes together. Add 1 tsp salt (or to taste) and 1 tsp flavourful masala. Stir fry for 2-3 minutes on low heat.
8. Squeeze lemon juice. Cook for 3-4 minutes till capsicums turn slightly soft. Serve.

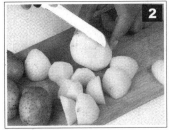

Sukhi Urad ki Dal

Serves 4

PRESSURE COOK TOGETHER
1 cup urad dhuli dal (split black beans) - soaked for ½ hour
½" piece ginger - very finely chopped
2 green chillies - very finely chopped
½ tsp haldi, 1¼ tsp salt
1 cup water

TADKA/TEMPERING
3-4 tbsp desi ghee or oil
1 big onion - finely chopped
1" piece ginger - cut into match sticks
1 big tomato - finely chopped
½ tsp chilli powder, ½ tsp garam masala
2 tbsp chopped coriander leaves to garnish

1. Clean, wash dal. Soak dal in water for ½ hour. Strain dal.
2. Pressure cook dal with 1 cup water and all the other ingredients. When the first whistle comes, slow down the fire and keep for 1 minute only.
3. Remove from fire. Open the cooker only after the pressure drops down. Keep aside.
4. At the time of serving, for the tempering, heat ghee. Add onions. Cook till light brown.
5. Add ginger match sticks and stir for a few seconds till onions turn brown.
6. Add tomatoes. Cook for 2-3 minutes.
7. Add ½ tsp chilli powder and ½ tsp garam masala. Cook for ½ minute.
8. Pour the hot oil or ghee over the dal. Mix gently.
9. Serve hot sprinkled with chopped coriander.

Kathal Laajawaab

Boiled kathal (not the usual fried) coated lightly with masala.

Serves 6

500 gm kathal (jack fruit)
¾ tsp salt, or to taste
1 tsp dhania powder
½ tsp garam masala, ¼ tsp haldi
1 tsp amchoor, ½ tsp red chilli powder
5 tbsp oil
seeds of 1 moti illaichi (brown cardamom) - crushed
1 tbsp green coriander

GRIND TOGETHER TO A PASTE
1 onions - chopped roughly
2 large tomato - chopped roughly
1 green chilli
1" piece ginger, 6-8 flakes garlic

1. Rub oil on your hands. Cut the whole big piece of kathal from the middle into two pieces. Remove skin. Cut widthwise from the centre of each piece. This way you get two big strips of kathal. Now further divide each strip into smaller pieces about 1" thickness, carefully to keep the shreds of the piece together . Then further divide into ½" thick pieces.
2. Boil 5 cups water with 2 tsp salt and ½ tsp haldi. Add kathal and boil uncovered for 7-8 minutes till a little soft. Keep it firm and crisp and do not over boil. Drain and keep aside.
3. Heat oil. Add onion-tomato paste and cook for 3-4 minutes. Add salt and all the masalas. Cook further for 5-7 minutes on low heat till oil separates.
4. Add the boiled kathal. Mix well gently and cook covered for 6-8 minutes on low heat till the vegetable blends well with the masala.
5. Sprinkle crushed illaichi. Mix. Serve hot garnished with chopped coriander.

Gobi De Danthal

Serves 3-4

danthal (stalks) of 4-5 small cauliflowers
1 large onion - chopped finely
1" piece ginger - chopped
2 tomatoes - chopped finely
1 green chilli - chopped
1 tsp dhania powder, ½ tsp garam masala
½ tsp red chilli powder
¾ tsp amchoor
1 tsp salt, or to taste
¼ tsp haldi
3-4 tbsp oil

1. Cut off the head of the cauliflower. Use it for subzi or paranthas as you like. From the stem (danthal), remove the side leaves, leaving 1-2 soft leaves at the top. Peel the hard stem a little from the lower end (the hard part). Cut each stalk into 4 long pieces.
2. Soak danthals very well in a pan full of hot water for 5-7 minutes. Wash well to remove the hidden dirt. Scrub well in between the side leaves.
3. Heat oil. Add onion and cook till light brown.
4. Add ginger and stir fry for a minute.
5. Add masalas - dhania powder, garam masala, red chilli powder, amchoor, salt and haldi. Cook for 2-3 minutes till the masala turns brown.

6. Add tomatoes and green chilli. Cook on medium flame for about 5 minutes, till the tomatoes are well blended and oil separates.
7. Add the danthals and stir fry for 2-3 minutes.
8. Cover and cook on low flame for 35-40 minutes.
9. Occasionally put 2-3 tbsp of water on the lid, which makes the water hot as it seeps in. Cook stirring occasionally till crisp tender. Do not overcook and make them too soft. Very soft danthals never taste nice.

Sukhe Matar Aloo

Serves 4

Picture on page 39

4 small sized potatoes - boiled
¾ cup boiled or frozen peas
1½ tbsp til (sesame seeds)
¾ tsp jeera (cumin seeds)
3 tbsp oil
1 large onion - chopped very finely
4-5 cashews - split into halves
10-15 kishmish - soaked in water
1 tsp salt, or to taste
¼ tsp haldi
½ tsp garam masala, ½ tsp red chilli powder, ½ tsp amchoor
2-3 tbsp chopped coriander
2-3 green chillies - whole
2 tsp lemon juice

1. Boil potatoes in salted water until just tender. They should feel soft when a knife is inserted. Do not over cook. (You may also pressure cook the potatoes for a quicker subzi or microwave the potatoes if you wish - 4 potatoes would take about 4 minutes on full power).
2. Peel and cut each potato widthwise into 2 equal halves.
3. Heat oil. Reduce heat. Add til and jeera. Wait till the til (sesame seeds) starts changing colour.
4. Add onions. Cook until onions turn light brown.
5. Add kaju. Stir-fry for a minute. Add kishmish.
6. Add salt, haldi, garam masala, red chilli powder and amchoor. Mix.
7. Add green chillies and fresh coriander. Cook for 1 minute.
8. Add 2-3 tbsp water.
9. Add the potatoes. Stir-fry gently for about 3 minutes on low heat, taking care not to break the potatoes.
10. Finally, add peas. Mix gently. Cook for 2 minutes stirring occasionally. Add lemon juice and mix well. Remove from fire. Serve hot.

Gur Waale Shalgam

A sweet and tangy vegetable.

Serves 2-3

½ kg shalgam (turnips)
1½ tsp gur (powdered) or shakkar
1" piece ginger - grated
1 green chilli - chopped
2 tbsp chopped coriander
1 tsp dhania powder, ½ tsp red chilli powder
½ tsp garam masala, ½ tsp salt, or to taste

1. Peel the shalgams and cut into 1" cubes (like potatoes).
2. Put in a pressure cooker with ½ cup water give 2 whistles. Remove from fire.
3. Heat 3 tbsp oil. Add ginger and green chillies. Let ginger turn light brown.
4. Add shalgam. Cook mashing occasionally till water dries and it looks like a halwah.
5. Add gur and masalas. Mix well for 2-3 minutes. Add coriander and serve.

Baingan Di Kachri

Crisp brinjal slices coated with wheat flour.

Serves 4

1 medium round baingan (brinjal) - washed & cut into thin slices (15 slices)
1 tsp kuti laal mirch (red chilli flakes)
4-5 tbsp atta (whole wheat flour)
3-4 tbsp oil for shallow frying

1. Sprinkle 1½ tsp salt on baingan ke slices, leave to sweat for 15-20 minutes. Drain out water. Pat dry.
2. Spread them on a plate. Sprinkle red chilli flakes and some atta on the slices. Overturn the slices and sprinkle more red chilli flakes and atta on the other side too. Keep aside till serving time.
3. At the time of serving, sprinkle ½ tsp salt on the baingan slices.
4. Heat 3-4 tbsp oil in a frying pan or a tawa. Fry 4-5 baingan slices at a time till crisp on both sides. Turn with the help of a chimta (tongs) or a knife to brown both sides. Serve.

CHAAWAL

Matar Vadi Wale Chaawal

Serves 4

1-2 vadis (of moong or urad dal)
1 cup shelled peas
1 cup basmati rice - soaked for 1 hour
4 tbsp oil
1 tsp jeera (cumin seeds)
2 moti illaichi (brown cardamoms)
4 laung (cloves)
1 tej patta (bay leaf)
1" piece ginger - cut into matchsticks
1¼ tsp salt, or to taste
juice of ½ lemon

1. Drain soaked rice and keep ready.
2. Heat oil in a heavy bottomed pan. Reduce flame. Add vadi and fry turning sides till well browned all over. Remove from oil and keep aside.
3. Heat remaining oil. Add jeera, moti illaichi, laung and tej patta.
4. When jeera turns golden, add ginger and peas. Fry for 1 minute.
5. Break vadi into small pieces.
6. Add rice and the broken vadis. Fry for 1 minute, stirring gently.
7. Add 2 cups water, salt and lemon juice. Boil. After one boil cover tightly and lower heat.
8. Cook for about 8-10 minutes, till all the water is used and the rice well cooked.

Aloo Gobhi Chaawal

Serves 4

3 cups boiled rice
1 medium cauliflower - broken into medium florets along with the stalk
1 potato - cut into 8 pieces
1" piece ginger - cut into thin match sticks
1 fresh thick red chilli (used for pickles) or green chilli - slit, deseeded and cut into thin long pieces
3 tbsp oil
1 tsp ginger paste
1 tsp jeera (cumin seeds)
2 onions - halved and cut into round, thin slices (semi circles)
½ tsp garam masala, 1 tsp salt or to taste, ½ tsp red chilli powder

1. Wash cauliflower florets & potato pieces. Soak them in 2-3 cups water with 2 tsp salt, for about 10 minutes. Remove from water & wipe dry with a kitchen towel.
2. Deep fry cauliflower florets in medium hot oil to a light golden brown colour.
3. Reduce flame and add potato pieces to oil. Deep fry on low flame till well browned and cooked. (Insert a knife in a piece of potato in oil to see if it has turned soft).
4. Heat 3 tbsp oil in a large kadhai or a non stick wok. Reduce flame.
5. Add jeera.
6. When it turns golden, add onions and stir till they turn light brown.
7. Add ginger paste. Mix.
8. Add ½ tsp garam masala, 1 tsp salt and ½ tsp red chilli powder. Mix.
9. Fluff the rice and add rice to the onions. Stir fry till well mixed.
10. Mix in the fried cauliflower, potatoes, ginger match sticks and green or red chilli pieces. Stir fry for a few minutes. Serve.

Cutting of cauliflower and potato

Tikha Subzi Pulao

Try it, it's spicy and delicious!

Serves 3-4

1 cup basmati rice (soaked for 15 minutes)
50 gms paneer - diced to get small squares (½ cup)
1 carrot - diced (cut into ½" pieces)
1 small capsicum - diced
2½ tsp salt, ½ tsp haldi powder
3½ tbsp lemon juice, 4 tbsp oil
1½ cup water and 1 cup milk

PASTE (makes ½ cup apporx.)
5 dried, red chillies - deseed and soak in water for 15-20 minutes
1 onion - chopped
6-7 large flakes garlic, 2 tsp chopped ginger
1 tbsp cumin seeds (jeera), 1 tsp saunf (fennel)
1" stick dalchini (cinnamon)
seeds of 2 moti illaichi (brown cardamom)
¼ tsp grated jaiphal (nutmeg), 1 tbsp saboot dhania (coriander seeds)
2 laung (cloves), 4 saboot kali mirch (black peppercorns)

1. For paste, roast all ingredients of the paste in a kadhai for 5 minutes or till fragrant.
2. Grind to a fine paste. Use little water if needed. Keep paste aside.
3. Mix 1½ cups of water with 1 cup milk. Keep aside.
4. Heat oil in a heavy bottomed kadhai or a saucepan (patila) with a well fitted lid. Add the prepared paste. Fry till aromatic and leaves oil.
5. Reduce heat, add ½ cup of milk mixture. Cook till nearly dry.
6. Add carrot. Stir fry for a minute.
7. Add salt, haldi, lemon juice, remaining milk, paneer, capsicum and the soaked rice. Give one boil.
8. Reduce heat and cook covered for 8-10 minutes or till all the water has dried and the rice is cooked. Serve hot garnished with lemon wedges and tomato slices.

Achaari Chana Pulao

Picture on page 2   *Serves 4*

1 cup rice - wash and leave in the strainer for 30 minutes
3 tbsp oil
¾ tsp jeera (cumin seeds), ¾ tsp kalonji (onion seeds), ¾ tsp saunf (fennel seeds)
1 onion - sliced
1 tsp finely chopped ginger
½ tsp garam masala
½ tsp red chilli powder
1½ tsp salt, or to taste
1 tbsp lemon juice
a few coriander leaves with a little stalk

SOAK TOGETHER
½ cup black channa (kale channe)
1 dalchini (cinnamon), 2-3 laung (cloves)
2 cups water
½ tsp salt

1. Soak channas overnight with all the given ingredients and pressure cook to give 1 whistle. Keep on low flame for 20 minutes.
2. Strain channas reserving the water. Measure the stock (water of the channas) and add enough water to make it upto 2 cups (double the volume of rice).
3. Heat oil in a heavy bottomed pan.
4. Reduce flame. Add jeera, kalonji and saunf. When jeera turns golden, add the sliced onion.
5. Stir fry till onions turn transparent.
6. Add ginger. Stir fry for 1 minute.
7. Add cooked channas, lemon juice, salt, garam masala and red chilli powder. Stir fry for 2 minutes.
8. Add rice. Mix. Add coriander leaves. Stir gently on low flame for 2 minutes.
9. Add the measured stock and water mixture. Boil.
10. Cover with a towel napkin and then with a well fitting lid. Cook on very low flame till done.
11. Fluff with a fork to let the steam escape so that the rice grains do not stick to each other. Serve hot with curd and a green salad.

Achaari Bhindi: Recipe on page 63, Anjeeri Gobhi: Recipe on page 62 ➤

Kesar waala Pulao

Serves 3-4

1 cup basmati rice - wash in 2-3 changes of water. Strain and let the rice be in the strainer for 30 minutes (do not soak)
¼ tsp kesar - roasted on a tawa for a few seconds and soaked in 2 tbsp warm water
4 tbsp oil, ½ tsp shah jeera (black cumin), 2 tej patta (bay leaves)
1 onion - cut into slices
8-10 almonds - split into two pieces, 1 tbsp kishmish
1 carrot - cut into round slices
¼ of a small flower - cut into small florets
10 french beans - cut into ½" pieces
½ cup leaves of poodina (mint)
1½ tsp salt, ½ tsp haldi, 1 tbsp lemon juice

PASTE (GRIND WITH A LITTLE WATER)
4 flakes garlic, ½" piece ginger
seeds of 4 chhoti illaichi (green cardamoms) & 1 moti illaichi (black cardamom)
2 laung, 2-3 saboot kali mirch, ½" piece dalchini
½ tsp jeera (cumin seeds)

1. Wash and strain rice. Let it be in the strainer for 30 minutes.
2. Grind all ingredients of the paste together with a little water to a paste. Keep this ginger-garlic-spice paste aside.
3. Heat oil in a heavy bottomed pan. Add shah jeera and tej patta. Wait for 1 minute till jeera crackles.
4. Add onion slices and stir till light brown.
5. Add almonds and kishmish. Saute for a few seconds.
6. Add all vegetables. Stir for 2-3 minutes.
7. Add the freshly ground ginger-garlic-spice paste and salt. Stir to mix well. Bhuno vegetables for 2 minutes with this paste.
8. Add rice and lemon juice. Mix.
9. Add the soaked kesar. Do not mix.
10. Add 2 cups warm water and poodina leaves. Boil.
11. Add haldi. Stir to mix. Reduce heat and cook covered till the water dries up, for about 14-15 minutes.
12. Serve rice with any raita of your choice.

Makki di Roti: Recipe on page 81, Sarson da Saag: Recipe on page 36

ROTI

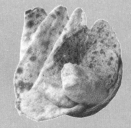

Poodina Parantha

Picture on cover   *Makes 6*

4 tbsp freshly chopped or dry poodina (mint leaves)
2 cups atta (whole wheat flour)
1 tsp ajwain (carom seeds)
2 tbsp oil
½ tsp salt
½ tsp red chilli powder

1. Mix atta with all ingredients except poodina. Add enough water to make a dough of rolling consistency.
2. Make walnut sized balls. Roll out to make a thick chappati.
3. Spread 1 tsp of ghee all over. Cut a slit from the outer edge till the centre.
4. Start rolling from the slit to form a cone.
5. Keeping the cone upright, press cone gently.
6. Roll out to a thick roti. Sprinkle poodina. Press with the belan (rolling pin).
7. Cook on a tawa, frying on both sides or apply some water on the back side of the parantha and stick it in a hot tandoor. Serve hot.

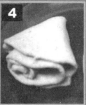

Gur ka Parantha

Serves 4

2 cups atta (whole wheat flour)
¾ cup water, approx.
ghee for frying

FILLING
½ cup powdered gur ki shakkar (jaggery powder)
2 tbsp chopped kaju
1 tbsp chopped kishmish
seeds of 2 moti illaichi (black cardamom) - crushed

1. Mix whole wheat flour with enough water to get a dough or rolling consistency. Knead well till smooth. Cover and keep aside for atleast 30 minutes.
2. Make 8 marble sized balls of the dough. Roll out 1 ball into a very thin round.
3. Sprinkle 2 tbsp gur on it. Sprinkle 1 tsp chopped kaju, ½ tsp chopped kishmish and some crushed illaichi seeds on it.
4. Roll out another ball into a very thin round and place it on the first round over the filling. Press the edges well to join. Gently roll out a little with the rolling pin (belan).
5. Carefully pick up the parantha and put it on a hot tawa (griddle). When the underside is cooked, turn to cook the other side.
6. Smear some ghee on the parantha. Trickle some ghee on the sides too, around the edges. Turn and brown both sides. Similarly make other paranthas. Serve.

Tandoori Roti

Makes 6-7

2 ½ cups atta (whole wheat flour)
1 cup water (approx.)
½ tsp salt
2-3 tbsp ghee

1. Keep ghee in the fridge for some time, so that it solidifies.
2. Make a soft dough with atta, salt and water. Keep aside for half an hour.
3. Divide the dough into 6 equal balls. Flatten each ball, roll out each into a round of 5" diameter.
4. Spread 1 tsp of solidified ghee. Sprinkle a teaspoon of dry flour on the ghee.
5. Make a slit, starting from any one end till almost to the other end, leaving just 1".
6. Start rolling from the slit, to form an even cone.
7. Keep the cone upright. Press a little from the middle to flatten slightly.
8. Roll out, to a diameter of 5", applying pressure only at the centre and not on the sides. Cook carefully in a heated tandoor till brown specs appear.

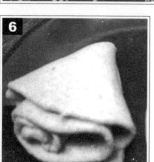

Amritsari Nan

Makes 6

2½ cups (250 gm) maida (plain flour)
½ cup hot milk
1 tsp baking powder
½ cup warm water (approx.)
½ tsp salt
10 badaam (almonds) - cut into long thin pieces (slivered)

1. Heat milk and put it in a big bowl. Add baking powder to the hot milk. Mix well and keep it aside for 1-2 minutes.
2. Sift maida and salt together. Add maida to the hot milk. Mix.
3. Knead to a dough with enough warm water.
4. Keep in a warm place for 3-4 hours.
5. Make 6-8 balls.
6. Roll out each ball to an oblong shape. Spread ghee all over. Fold one side (lengthways) a little, so as to overlap an inch of the nan. Press on the joint with the belan (rolling pin).
7. Sprinkle some chopped almonds. Press with a rolling pin (belan). Pull one side of the nan to give it a pointed end like the shape of the nan.
8. Apply some water on the back side of the nan. Stick in a hot tandoor.
9. Cook till nan is ready. Spread butter on the ready nan and serve hot.

Makki di Roti

Makes 6-7   *Picture on page 76*

2 cups makki ka atta (maize flour)
hot water - to knead, ghee for frying

1. Sieve the flour. Knead gently with hot water to a soft dough. Do not knead the dough too much in advance.
2. Tear an old polythene bag into two halves. Keep one piece of polythene on the chakla (rolling platform). Put one ball of the kneaded dough on the polythene. Cover with the other piece of polythene, such that there is a plastic cover above and beneath the ball.
3. Roll carefully to a slightly thick roti.
4. Cook roti on both sides on a tawa. Add some ghee and fry both sides on low flame. Serve hot with sarson ka saag.

Quick Peethi Poori

Makes 12

1 cup atta (whole wheat flour), ½ tsp salt
1 tsp oil or melted ghee
½ tsp salt
¼ cup urad dal - soaked for 2 hours and coarsely ground to get peethi
or ½ cup ready made dal ki peethi
1 tsp suji (semolina)
1 tsp kuti laal mirch (red chilli flakes), ¼ tsp ajwain (carom seeds)

1. Sift flour and ½ tsp salt together and rub in melted ghee or oil.
2. Knead to a little stiff dough with about ¾-1 cup water and set aside.
3. Mix dal ki peethi with ½ tsp salt, 1 tsp kuti laal mirch, ¼ tsp ajwain, 1 tsp suji.
4. Divide dough into small balls and roll out the balls into small poories.
5. Spread 1 tsp full peethi on the rolled out poori with the spoon. The peethi is spread on the outside of the puri instead of stuffing it within.
6. Heat oil, drop the rolled poories gently into it **with the peethi side down in the oil,** so that the dal gets cooked in the hot oil.
7. Press the sides of the poori with a perforated frying spoon and make the poori swell up. Turn. Fry till golden brown and crisp. Drain on brown paper.

Note: The peethi can be stuffed inside the poori also.

Bhature

Picture on page 40

Makes 8

2 cups maida (plain flour)
1 cup suji (semolina)
½ tsp soda-bicarb
½ tsp salt, ½ tsp sugar
½ cup sour curd
oil for deep frying

1. Soak suji in water, which is just enough to cover it. Keep aside for 10 minutes.
2. Sift salt, soda and maida in a paraat. Add sugar, soaked suji and curd.
3. Knead with enough warm water to make a dough of rolling consistency.
4. Knead again with greased hands till the dough is smooth.
5. Brush the dough with oil. Keep the dough in a greased polythene and keep it in a warm place for 3-4 hours.
6. Make 8-10 balls. Roll each ball to an oblong shape. Deep fry in hot oil. Serve.

ACHAAR & CHUTNEY

Instant Khatti Mithi Chutney

Serves 6

1 tbsp amchoor (dried mango powder)
3 tbsp sugar or shakkar (gur)
½ tsp roasted jeera (cumin seeds)
¼ tsp red chilli powder, ¼ tsp salt, ¼ tsp garam masala
¼ cup water

1. Mix all ingredients together in a small heavy bottomed pan.
2. Cook on low flame, till all the ingredients dissolve properly and the chutney gets the right consistency. Remove from fire.

Amm Da Achaar

1.5 kg raw mangoes (kachhe amm)
150 gm salt, 50 gms red chilli powder, 25 gms haldi powder
50 gms saunf (aniseeds) - dry roast lightly on a tawa (gridle)
50 gms methi daana (fenugreek seeds)
30 gms kalonji (onion seeds)
2 cups mustard oil (sarson ka tail)

1. Wash mangoes. Wipe with a clean cloth. Cut into 1" pieces.
2. Heat the oil in a kadhai. Remove from fire and transfer to a large pan. Cool oil.
3. Add salt, red chilli powder, haldi, saunf, methi daana and kalonji to the oil.
4. Add the mango slices to the masala oil. Mix well.
5. Fill into a jar. Keep jar in the sun, shaking it once daily.
6. To preserve the pickle for a longer time, heat some more oil and cool it.
7. Pour oil in the jar of pickle to cover the mango slices.

Dahi Poodina Chutney

Serves 6

GRIND TOGETHER
½ cup poodina (mint), ½ cup hara dhania (green coriander)
2 green chillies
½ onion, 2 flakes garlic
a pinch of kala namak, ¼ tsp bhuna jeera, salt to taste

ADD LATER
1½ cups curd - hang for 15 minutes
1 tsp oil

1. Wash coriander and mint leaves.
2. Grind coriander, mint, green chillies, onion and garlic with a little water to a paste.
3. Beat curd well till smooth.
4. To the hung curd, add the green paste, oil, kala namak, bhuna jeera and salt to taste. Serve with tandoori food.

Sirke Waale Pyaaz

Serves 4-6

12-13 small onions
½ cup white vinegar
½ cup water
1 tsp salt
½ tsp red chilli powder

1. Peel onions. Make a cross slit on each onion on the top.
2. Place in a bowl. Sprinkle salt and chilli powder on them and rub well.
3. Boil water and vinegar together in a pan. Remove from fire.
4. Pour the hot vinegar water over the onions in the bowl.
5. When the vinegar cools a little, transfer the onions and vinegar into a clean bottle. Keep in the refrigerator.
6. Use after a day.

Note: A few ginger match sticks and green chillies can also be added.

Gobi Shalgam Da Achaar

2½ kg - gobi, carrots and shalgam (all 3 vegetables mixed together)
100 gm garlic - ground to a paste
100 gm ginger - ground to paste
100 gm rai powder
3-4 tsp haldi
100 gms red chillies (for a hot pickle, add more chillies)
500 gm gur (jaggery)
2 cups (500 ml) vinegar
500 gm mustard oil
25 gm kasoori methi (dried fenugreek leaves)

1. Peel carrots and shalgam (turnips). Cut carrots into fingers, shalgam into round slices and gobi (cauliflower) into medium sized florets.
2. Boil water in a big pan. Add vegetables. Remove from fire immediately. Let the vegetables be in the hot water for ½ hour. Keep aside.
3. After ½ hour remove the vegetables from the water with a slotted spoon and dry them on a clean cloth in the shade.
4. Next day, heat oil to smoking point, reduce flame. Add garlic paste and fry till light golden in colour.
5. Add ginger paste & fry till light brown. Remove from fire.
6. Add salt, rai powder, kasoori methi, red chilli powder and haldi to the ginger-garlic mixture.
7. Smear the dried vegetables kept in a large pan, with this masala and transfer them in a jar.
8. In a clean dry pan heat vinegar, add gur to it and cook till gur dissolves. Strain it, cool and add it to the pickle in the jar. Shake well so that it mixes evenly with the vegetables.
9. Keep the pickle in the sun for 4-5 days.

Note:

1. If you want the pickle to be sweet, reduce the chillies and increase the gur according to taste.
2. If you like the pickle to be soft, boil the vegetables for 2-3 minutes and then remove from fire.

MITHA (SWEETS)

Anjeeri Chenna Kulfi

The khoya is substituted with low fat paneer. Anjeer adds a different touch to the kulfi.

Serves 3

2½ cups milk
2 tbsp sugar
½ cup finely grated paneer
8 anjeers - roughly chopped
1 tbsp badam- chopped
2 tbsp cornflour, 3 tbsp milk

1. Dissolve cornflour in 3 tbsp milk. Keep aside.
2. Heat 2½ cups milk with sugar. Boil and keep on fire for about 20- 25 minutes, till reduced to half the quantity. Add crushed illaichi seeds.
3. Add the cornflour paste to the boiling milk, stirring continuously.
4. Continue boiling, by lowering the flame, for about 2-3 minutes.
5. Add paneer, anjeer and almonds. Check sugar. Remove from fire. Cool. Let it come to room tempertaure.
6. Churn the prepared milk mixture in a mixie.
7. Fill in clean kulfi moulds and leave to set in the freezer for 6-8 hours.

Chana Dal & Khajur Halwa

Serves 4-5

250 gm khajur (dates) - deseeded & chopped
¾ cup channe ki dal
2½ cups milk
½ cup melted desi ghee
6-8 badaam (almonds) - chopped, 1 tbsp sugar
seeds of 3-4 chhoti illaichi (green cardamoms) - crushed

1. Wash and soak dal with enough water to cover. Keep aside for 30 minutes. Soak the chopped dates in ½ cup hot milk and keep aside.

2. Drain the water from the dal. Put it in a heavy bottomed kadhai. Add 2 cups milk to the dal. Keep on fire. Bring to a boil. Cook for about 20 minutes or till dal turns soft and about ½ cup milk remains.

3. Remove dal from fire and let it cool down.

4. Churn the dates along with the milk in which they were soaked to a paste. Remove from mixer to a bowl.

5. Churn the dal also along with the milk to a paste. Keep aside.

6. Heat ½ cup ghee in a clean kadhai. Add almonds. Stir for 2 minutes till golden.

7. Add the dal paste to the ghee and stir to mix well. Add the date paste also. Stir to mix well. Stir or bhuno the halwah on medium flame for about 10 minutes or till ghee separates.

8. Add sugar and illaichi powder and mix well till sugar dissolves. Serve hot.

Jalebi Te Rabri

Serves 8

JALEBI
1 cup maida, 1 tbsp besan, ¼ tsp (level) soda bicarb
½ tbsp oil
½ cup thick curd
¾ cup warm water
oil or ghee for frying

SYRUP
1¼ cups sugar, ¾ cup water
2-3 pinches orange-red colour

1. Sieve maida, besan and soda. Add curd and oil. Add enough warm water (about ¾ cup) to make a batter of a soft dropping consistency.
2. Beat batter well till smooth. Cover and keep aside for 30-40 minutes.
3. Heat oil or ghee in a frying pan till medium hot. Put the batter in a piping bag and make circles within circle, starting from the outside.
4. Reduce heat. Fry them golden brown on low heat on both sides, turning carefully with a pair of tongs (chimta). Remove from oil, drain excess oil and keep aside.
5. For the syrup, boil sugar, water and colour in a kadhai. After the first boil keep on low flame for 5-7 minutes till a stringy syrup is attained.
6. At serving time, dip 4-5 jalebis at a time in the hot syrup for 1 minute, take out and serve them hot with rabri.

RABRI
4 cups full cream milk
75 gm khoya - grated, (½ cup)
2 tbsp sugar
6-8 pistas - chopped
3 chhoti illaichi (green cardamoms) - powdered
rose petals or silver sheet (varq)

1. Boil milk in a heavy bottomed kadhai. Add khoya and sugar.
2. Simmer on low-medium heat for about 40-45 minutes, scraping the sides, till the quantity is reduced to almost half and the mixture turns thick with a thick pouring consistency. Remove from fire. The rabri turns thick on keeping.
3. Add some chopped pistas and cardamom powdered into the mixture.
4. Transfer to a serving dish and garnish with pistas and rose petals.
5. Chill and serve plain by itself or with jalebis or with some fruit.

Seb (apple) ka Meetha

Serves 8

2 apples - grated with the peel

SUGAR SYRUP
¼ cup sugar, ¼ cup water
seeds of 4-5 chhoti illaichi (green cardamoms) - crushed
2 drops kewra essence

KESARI MILK
3 cups milk
¼ tsp saffron (kesar)
3 tbsp sugar
1 cup milk mixed with 2 tbsp cornflour

OTHER INGREDIENTS
1 apple - grated with the peel
4-5 almonds and 4-5 kishmish - chopped
seeds of 2-3 chhoti illaichi (green cardamoms) - crushed

1. For the sugar syrup, put sugar, water and illaichi in a kadhai. Bring to a boil. Simmer on low heat for 2-3 minutes.
2. To the syrup, add 2 grated apples. Cook for 3-4 minutes till dry. Add kewra essence and mix well.
3. For the kesari milk, boil milk with kesar in a clean kadhai.
4. Add sugar and reduce heat. Simmer for 15 minutes till it is reduced to about ½ the quantity. Do not let it get thick.
5. Add cornflour dissolved in milk. Bring to a boil, stirring constantly. Cook for 2-3 minutes on low heat till thick.
6. Add the sweetened apples. Cook till quite thick. Remove from fire.
7. Grate 1 apple and spread a layer of grated apple at the base of a medium size serving dish.
8. Pour the apples in milk over the apple layer in the dish and spread. Sprinkle some illaichi powder and chopped nuts. Keep in the fridge for 2-3 hours to set.

Kesar waale Mitthe Chaawal

Serves 4

1 cup Basmati rice - must be soaked for 1 hour
a few strands of kesar (saffron)
1 cup sugar
3 tbsp desi ghee
4 chhoti illaichi (green cardamoms)
3 laung (cloves)
a small piece of fresh or dried coconut - cut into thin pieces, optional
6-8 badam (almonds) - blanched & shredded
1 tbsp kishmish (raisins) - soaked in some water

1. Mix ¾ cup water and 1 cup sugar in a small pan. Add kesar. Keep on fire to boil. Stir in between. Remove from fire as soon as syrup boils. Keep aside.
2. Heat ghee in a big heavy bottomed pan. Reduce heat. Add chhoti illaichi and laung. Stir fry for a few seconds till illaichi changes colour.
3. Add coconut, almonds and kishmish. Stir till kishmish swells.
4. Discard water and add rice. Mix gently so that the rice grains do not break.
5. Add 1¼ cups water. Boil.
6. Reduce flame. Keep a tawa under the pan of rice as soon as it starts to boil to reduce the heat further.
7. Cook for about 10 minutes till the water gets absorbed.
8. Add the kesar waala sugar syrup. Mix lightly with a fork. Cover and cook further on low heat till rice is done and the syrup gets absorbed.

Chhuare Te Chaawal Di Kheer

Serves 6

1 kg full cream milk
2 chhuare (dried dates) - soaked overnight or for at least ½ hour in
warm water & chopped finely
¼ cup uncooked rice - soaked for ½ hour
¼ cup sugar
3-4 chhoti illaichi (green cardamoms) - powdered
a few almonds - blanched, to garnish

1. Boil milk in a heavy bottomed kadhai. Drain rice and add to the boiling milk. Add the finely chopped chhuaras also.
2. Cook on low medium flame for 35-40 minutes, stirring frequently, till the rice is well cooked and blends well with the milk. Keep mashing the rice grains and the chhuaras also, in between. Keep scraping the sides of the kadhai too. Remove from fire when thick.
3. Add sugar and illaichi powder. Mix and transfer to a serving dish.
4. Garnish with chopped almonds. Serve hot or cold.

Mithae Jauley

A very popular Punjabi dessert. It made on all happy occasions.

Serves 8-10

250 gms roasted Jauley (small, thick, vermicelli)
6 tbsp pure ghee
1 cup sugar
3 cups water
½-1 cup mixed chopped dry fruits (cashewnuts, kishmish, almonds etc.)

1. In a kadhai heat ghee. Add seviyaan (vermicelli) and fry to a rich brown colour. Do not over brown.
2. Mix sugar and water together in a separate pan. Give one boil and mix till all the sugar dissolves. Remove from fire.
3. Add sugar syrup to the seviyaan in the kadhai and boil.
4. Add dry fruit. Cover and cook till they turn soft and dry.
5. Serve hot with rabri or cold thick rice kheer or just by themselves.

Note: If using long, thin seviyaan, break the seviyaan into 3"-4" pieces. Do not cover while cooking these.

Coco Gulla

Picture on facing page   Serves 4

4 readymade white rasgullas - cut each into 2 pieces
¼ tsp kesar dissolved in 3 tbsp warm milk for 10 minutes
2½ cup milk, 1 tbsp sugar
1 packet coconut powder (maggie)
2 tbsp cornflour mixed with ½ cup milk
a few almonds/ pistas - chopped, to garnish

Cutting of Rasgulla

1. Boil milk in a heavy bottomed kadhai.
2. Cook on low medium flame for 15- 20 minutes, stirring frequently, Keep scraping the sides of the pan too. Remove from fire when thick.
3. Add coconut powder, dissolved kesar and sugar. Mix
4. Add cornflour paste & mix well sirring for few seconds. Remove from fire. Cool.
5. Add small halved rasgullas, mix. Keep aside in the fridge till serving time. Garnish with chopped almonds. Serve cold.

Anjeeri Halwa

Picture on page 3   Serves 6

200 gms anjeer (figs) - soaked in 3 cup hot water for 15 minutes
5 tbsp atta, 4 tbsp oil/ghee

CARAMEL SUGAR SYRUP
5 tbsp sugar, 3 tbsp oil

1. Soak anjeer in 3 cups hot water for 15 minutes.
2. Strain and reserve the water. Keep anjeer-water aside.
3. Grind the anjeer without water to a paste. Keep aside.
4. Heat 4 tbsp oil or ghee. Add atta and cook stirring on low heat till golden, for about 3-4 minutes.
5. Add anjeer paste and stir again on low heat for about 5 minutes. Keep aside.
6. In a clean, big kadhai, heat 3 tbsp oil and 5 tbsp sugar. Stir till sugar melts and turns golden. Remove from fire.
7. Add the anjeer water. Stir on low heat till it boils. Keep on fire till the syrup feels sticky between the sugar and thumb.
8. Remove syrup from fire.
9. Add syrup to anjeer paste and stir till semidry. Do not dry too much. Serve hot with rabri given on page 88.

Nita Mehta's BEST SELLERS (Vegetarian)

 Low Calorie **SNACKS**

 Chatpati **CHAAT**

 Vegetarian **SANDWICHES**

 **THAI** Vegetarian Cookery

 Vegetarian **SOUPS**

 Vegetarian **SALADS**

 Taste of **DELHI**

 **EVERYDAY** Khaana

 **Dal & Roti**

 **Desserts Puddings**

 **MUGHLAI** Vegetarian Khaana

 **Green Vegetables**

 **Vegetarian Dishes**

 **MENUS** from around the world

 **CONTINENTAL** Vegetarian Cookery

 **Eggless Desserts**

 Indian **LOW FAT**

 Vegetarian **CURRIES**

 **QUICK MEALS**

 More **PANEER**

 **INDIAN** Vegetarian

 **NEW CHINESE**

 **NEW MICROWAVE**

 **MICROWAVE** Vegetarian Cookery

Nita Mehta's BEST SELLERS (Vegetarian)

SUBZIYAAN

FOOD from around the **WORLD**

QUICK Vegetarian Cooking

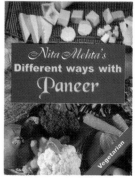

Different ways with **PANEER**

Vegetarian **MICROWAVE** Cookbook

Great **INDIAN** Cooking

EVERYDAY Cooking

Vegetarian **SNACKS**

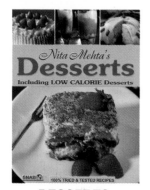

DESSERTS Including Low Calorie Desserts

VEGETARIAN Wonders

Perfect Vegetarian Cookery

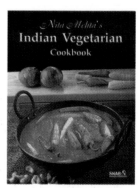

Indian Vegetarian Cookbook